1/05   Queit   19.76

MARY WOLLSTONECRAFT
AND THE RIGHTS OF WOMEN

World Writers

MARY WOLLSTONECRAFT
AND THE RIGHTS OF WOMEN

Calvin Craig Miller

MORGAN
REYNOLDS
Incorporated

Greensboro

Mary Wollstonecraft and the Rights of Women

Copyright © 1999 by Calvin Craig Miller

Library of Congress Cataloging-in-Publication Data
Miller, Calvin Craig, 1954
  Mary Wollstonecraft and the rights of women / Calvin Craig Miller. — 1st ed.
    p. cm. — (World writers)
  Includes bibliographical references and index.
  ISBN   1-883846-41-2
    1. Wollstonecraft, Mary, 1759-1797. 2. Women authors, English—18th century—
Biography. 3. Feminists—Great Britain—Biography. I. Title   II. Series.
PR5841.W8Z7565   1999
828' .609—dc21
[b]

                                                                99-13519
                                                                      CIP

Printed in the United States of America
First Edition

Contents

Mary Wollstonecraft

Chapter One

"I must have first place or none"

Growing up, Mary Wollstonecraft often felt like the loneliest girl living in her dreary neighborhood of Spitalfields, London. Her parents, Elizabeth and Edward John, lavished attention on her older brother, Ned, who was born in 1757, two years before Mary. She was left to fend for herself, or to trail after her mother and Ned, begging for attention and growing more and more angry as she was ignored.

Eventually, Mary learned to entertain herself. She played alone in the small, shadowed yard behind the Wollstonecraft house. She talked to herself as she performed all the roles in stories she made up in her head. As she grew older, her mother gave her more and more chores to do, and while she swept or scrubbed or mopped, Mary imagined herself living adventures in exotic lands. Any place would be brighter and cleaner and better than Spitalfields. The working-class neighborhood of London was a place where houses huddled close to one another. Smells from the neighbors' cook stoves drifted through the narrow streets; watchdogs growled menacingly; buckets of waste were tossed through windows into the streets. Boys trained dogs and roosters to fight, and fought themselves, in the courtyards and alleys.

The Wollstonecrafts could have lived in better circumstances if Mary's father had worked harder at his trade as a maker of handkerchiefs. Mary's grandfather had worked very hard and had acquired some property. Born in 1688, Edward Wollstone-craft came to Spitalfields from Lancashire. He worked as a silk weaver. Throughout his career, Edward Wollstonecraft saved his money and invested wisely. He bought three blocks of houses to rent. The rental houses would provide much of the family's income for two generations. By the time Grandfather Wollstonecraft had reached his sixties, he had accumulated enough wealth to be able to call himself a "gentleman."

Edward's oldest son, Edward John Wollstonecraft, who was to become Mary's father, worked seven years for his father as an apprentice. But Edward John Wollstonecraft lacked his father's patience, thrift, and willingness to work hard. Edward John preferred to spend his time at sporting events, gambling, and drinking.

Edward John married Elizabeth Dickson, a quiet country girl from a good family in the County Denegal in Ireland. Ned was the first-born. Mary was born on April 27, 1759. The family's second son, Henry Woodstock Wollstonecraft, was born in 1761 but died before his first birthday. The tragedy shocked Grandfather Wollstonecraft so badly that he bought his son's family a farm near Epping in the countryside. The days spent on the Epping farm were the happiest of Mary's childhood.

Elizabeth continued to have babies. Eliza was born in 1763;

King George II reigned over the British empire when Mary Wollstonecraft was born in 1759.

Everina in 1765 and a second son named James in 1768. The family's youngest, Charles, was born in 1770.

Forced to compete for affection in a large family, Mary early on began to feel jealousy. Mary's parents made it clear that they expected great things from Ned and not much from the girls. While Ned was sent to a good school, Mary had to learn to read from a woman hired to look after the children. Even so, she became good at reading and at expressing herself. She made up songs and held imaginary conversations with angels.

In February of 1765, Grandfather Wollstonecraft died. His will provided enough money to pay for his own grand funeral. Then he split the remainder of his estate into thirds. One third went to his daughter by his first marriage, a middle-aged woman whose children were grown. The second went to Mary's father. The final third was left to little Ned. Not a penny went to the Wollstonecraft girls.

Ned became cocky about his role as the favored child. Mary found it hard to keep her anger bottled up. She was pretty, with red curly hair, but her stress began to show in her face. She frowned and glared, unable to give words to the inner fury she felt toward her brother Ned.

Her resentment extended to other family members as well. She scorned her mother for her docility, her father for his laziness and drinking. But she felt a natural protectiveness toward the younger members of the family. She thought of herself as the family leader and provider. This was a role she often played in later years.

Her grandfather's will did make life happier for Mary in one way. The Wollstonecrafts used part of the money to buy another farm and to leave Spitalfields. They were also able to collect money regularly from the Primrose Street rentals. They lived by wealthier neighbors, such as the Goscoynes, who held influence in politics. Living in the countryside, Mary developed her powers of observation by intently watching the insects, birds and small animals. Her love of animals grew as well, another trait she would keep throughout her life.

This period of prosperity was short-lived, however. Her father's bad habits soon outstripped the family's ability to pay for them. He wanted to live like a country gentleman and to waste away his days at the horse track and taverns. He simply did not have the disposition of a farmer. Soon, the money and property were gone.

In 1768, the Wollstonecrafts loaded their belongings into a train of coaches and rumbled away up the Old North Road, to yet another farm in Beverly. Their house was pretty and overlooked a huge monastery on one side and a farmers market, called Wednesday Market, on the other. Mary soon discovered another playground called Westwood, where wildlife flourished amid the tall trees. Ned went to a grammar school, with a well-stocked library, as his parents prepared him for the practice of law.

Mary was educated in a village school, which did not have as many resources as Ned's school. Even so, Mary loved her school and learned her lessons well.

Mary soon met a girl who would become her best friend. Jane Arden was the daughter of a philosopher who lectured on science in Germany. Mr. Arden encouraged his daughters to learn, and established an open-minded atmosphere in his house. When she could not see Jane, Mary wrote her letters. So doing, she sharpened her writing skills and learned to convey passion through words.

Mary's affection turned to anger when she discovered that Jane had begun to spend time with another friend. At the age of sixteen Mary wrote Jane a letter:

"I once thought myself worthy of your friendship," she wrote. "I thank you for bringing me to a right sense of myself. When I have been at your house with Miss J----, the greatest respect has been paid to her: everything handed to her first; in short as if she were a superior being. Your Mama too behaved with more politeness to her."

Jane tried to make things right with Mary, but it was not an easy task. Denied what she considered proper affection from her own mother and father, Mary tried to find it with other families and from her friends. "I am a little singular in my thought of love and friendship," Mary wrote. "I must have first place or none . . . I cannot bear a slight from those I love."

Mary's father often returned from the racetracks broke and angry and drunk. He often turned his unpredictable and wild rages against Mary's mother. While Mary did not enjoy a warm relationship with her mother, she appointed herself the family's protector. Some girls might have cowered under such a bully as Edward John. Mary did not. She waited up when he stayed out late, sometimes sleeping near the steps. When her father arrived home in one of his dark moods and began assaulting her mother, Mary would throw her body between them so that some of the blows fell upon her instead.

Edward John packed up his family again in 1774. They moved to Hoxton, a small, ugly village north of London. Edward John tried another series of investments, but they did not go well. Ned came of age and was sent to a London solicitor for an apprenticeship of five or six years, the only way to learn the profession of law at the time.

Her father's drunkenness and lack of skill in financial matters led him deeper into rage and abuse. Mary longed to escape her dreary circumstances by leaving home. She started visiting an old couple called the Clares. Mary found warmth in the Clares' home, but not the kind of companionship she craved, from a girl her own age. One day the Clares introduced Mary to a young woman named Frances Blood, whom everyone called Fanny.

Fanny made a lasting first impression on Mary. Years later, she wrote about their meeting in a book of fiction. She described Fanny Blood as "a young woman of slender and elegant form, and eighteen years of age." Before their first meeting was over, Mary "had taken, in her heart, the vows of an eternal friendship."

Fanny had a lovely singing voice and also drew well. Mary even admired her for her handwriting, which was more elegant and ordered than Mary's hurried scrawl. It pleased Mary all the more that Fanny did not waver in her friendship or place rivals above her, as Jane Arden had. The two had no serious quarrels. Mary wrote Jane that she had made "a friend, whom I love better than all the world beside, a friend to whom I am bound by every tie of gratitude and inclination: to live with this friend is the height of my ambition, and indeed it is the most rational wish I could make, as her conversation is not more agreeable than improving. I could dwell forever on her praises, and you would not wonder at it, if you knew the many favors she has conferred on me, and the many valuable qualifications which she possesses; she has a masculine understanding, and sound judgment, yet she has every feminine virtue."

Unlike Jane Arden, Fanny did not enjoy many advantages over Mary. Mr. Blood did not provide for his family either. Fanny sold her drawings to help earn money for her family's upkeep. Mrs. Blood sewed, working from four in the morning until dark. At seventeen, Mary observed how little society helped women to provide for themselves.

Mary's father decided on yet another move, this time to Wales. The move separated her from Fanny, but Mary found Wales beautiful. The Wollstonecrafts lived in the village of Laugharne, near the mouth of the Towy river. Streams and rivers cut through towering hills and fishermen paddled by in light, round boats. A ruined castle of the middle ages brooded over the small town. Birds that Mary had never seen before flew through the skies. She listened to beautiful harp music from a musician who frequented a nearby inn.

But the beauty of the picturesque town could not heal the pain Mary felt at separating from Fanny. Then the family was forced to move again. But this time they went to the village of Walworth, near the Bloods' home. Mary was eighteen now, the oldest child still at home. She asked for a room of her own and a place to study.

Even with a room, Mary found living at home increasingly unbearable. The only thing keeping her there was a sense of duty. But Ned had already made it clear that he would provide little or nothing to his family when he started his law practice. Mary wondered why she should do more. She wanted to strike out on her own.

In 1778, at the age of nineteen, Mary accepted one of the few positions that allowed a young woman the means to make a living. She became the companion of an older woman named Mrs. Dawson, who lived in Bath. She would have preferred a position that could use her writing talents, but she was determined to leave home. She was going to make an independent life for herself, regardless of what society decreed.

Chapter Two

"Pain and disappointment have constantly attended me"

Mary stepped down from the coach at Bath, rumpled and weary from the twenty-four hour coach ride from Walworth. She went straight to the house of Mrs. Dawson on Milsom Street, ready for the challenge. Mrs. Dawson was a difficult employer whose exacting demands had forced many other young women to leave her. She would meet her match in Mary, whose determination had been forged in battles with her father.

At first, life with Mrs. Dawson did not turn out as badly as Mary had feared. Mrs. Dawson allowed Mary some liberties. She gave Mary time off to visit her family and Fanny Blood, who lived nearby.

In the year 1778, Bath was one of the most popular resort towns in Europe. The mineral content of its water was thought to have healing properties. The sick came to be cured. The rich came to relax, mingle and be seen in the fashionable bathing spots. These visitors enriched Bath. But the airs of the well-to-do and all of those who hung around them disgusted Mary.

Bath was beautiful, though. Hills towered over one side of the town to form a natural amphitheater, and the land stepped away from the hills in broad terraces. Mary wrote of her street, Milsom, that "whether in or out of the Season . . . is the very magnet of Bath, and if there is any company or movement in the city, Milsom Street is the pulse of it."

Mary still longed for the time she and Fanny might live together. She was fearful when a courtship developed between Fanny and a merchant named Hugh Skeys. Mary had been through a brief romance of her own with an Oxford clergyman named Joshua Waterhouse. The brief flirtation did not last. She found Waterhouse to be vain and overbearing. She preferred the company of female friends. Jane's father was now living in Bath as well. Seeing his advertisement for tutoring services in the newspaper one day, she decided to pay a call to Jane and to renew their friendship.

Mary wrote both of her friends when she could not see them. She was critical of the lifestyle of rich, idle young women, and her letters helped her learn how to express her objections forcefully. She particularly looked down on women who thought and talked of nothing but clothes, as Mrs. Dawson's nieces did. She also poked fun at how they were excited by catching a glimpse of the Prince of Wales. "All the damsels set their caps at him, and you would smile to hear how the poor girls he condescends to take notice of are pulled to pieces," she wrote Jane. "The withered old maids sagaciously hint their fears, and kindly remark that they always thought them forward things: you would suppose a smile or a look of his has something fatal in it, and that a maid could not look at him and remain pure."

Although she was proud of doing a good job as Mrs. Dawson's companion, Mary suffered periods of depression and self-doubt.

She wrote of herself as old and wrinkled, though she was not yet twenty. She dressed plainly, and considered such dress a virtue. She doubted she would ever attract a husband, and questioned whether she would want one, in light of the examples set by her father and Mr. Blood. Mary was beginning to settle into the pattern that molded her life—elation and accomplishment, followed by depression. At times, she found her only strength in religious faith: "Pain and disappointment have constantly attended me since I left Beverly," she wrote Jane. "I do not however repine at the dispensations of Providence, for my philosophy as well as my religion will ever teach me to look on misfortunes as blessings, which like a bitter potion is disagreeable to the palate tho' 'tis grateful to the Stomach—I hope mine have not been thrown away on me, but that I am the wiser and better for them."

Adding to her gloom was Mary's separation from her family. She had worked hard for her independence, but still felt a sense of responsibility toward her younger brothers and sisters. Mary rebuked Eliza for sending no news of their mother: "The happiness of my family is nearer my heart than you imagine—perhaps too near for my own health and peace of mind," she wrote. " . . . You don't say a word of my mother. I take it for granted that she is well—tho' of late she has not even desired to be remembered to me. Some time or the other, in this world or a better, she may be convinced of my regard—and then may think I deserve not to be thought so harshly of."

Mary must have sensed that something was wrong. Soon she was summoned with the news that her mother was seriously ill.

She hurried to Enfield, where the family had moved since she left for Bath. There she found her mother lying in bed in pain, her limbs swollen. She suffered from what people at that time called "dropsy," a swelling from accumulated fluids. Many diseases—heart congestion and cancer among them—could have caused it. It soothed Elizabeth Wollstonecraft to see Mary arrive. Mary stayed by her mother's bedside as death approached. Then, on April 19, 1782, Elizabeth said her last words. "A little patience and all will be over," she whispered.

Mary watched as her mother breathed her last breath. She could not get her mother's dying words out of her head. "A little patience"? Mary vowed she would never be so patient!

After her mother's death, Mary did not return to Mrs. Dawson's. She went instead to live with Fanny Blood and her family at Walham Green.

Mary had at last achieved her dream of living with Fanny, but the experience was not what she had hoped. There were too many people crammed in a small house. It reminded Mary of her childhood. Then she discovered that Fanny had consumption, what we today call tuberculosis. Mary had read some medical books and knew the disease to be life threatening. She did not tell Fanny, but simply hoped for the best. Meanwhile, she put up with visits from the detested Hugh Skeys, Fanny's suitor.

While Mary struggled to make a life more independent than most young women, her younger sisters were all too ready to settle into traditional molds. Her youngest sister Eliza became pregnant and accepted a marriage of necessity. In October of

1782, Eliza married a twenty-one year old boatbuilder from Bermondsy in the county of Surrey. The groom's name was Meredith Bishop. Eliza bore a daughter a few weeks after the wedding. The baby was named Mary. After her baby's birth, Eliza fell into a deep depression. When Mary arrived at the Bishops' home, she found her sister in a rattled state. Eliza spoke of having been treated badly by her new husband.

Eliza's condition deeply troubled Mary. She wrote to Everina about Eliza's troubles: "She has not had a violent fit of frenzy since I saw you, but her mind is in a most unsettled state," Mary wrote. "A number of wild whims float on her imagination, and fall from her unconnectedly . . . She seems to think she has been very ill used, and in short, till I see some more favorable symptoms, I shall only suppose that her malady has assumed a new and more distressing appearance."

Eliza's new husband also fell sick. Even through the haze of his fever, Meredith Bishop began to suspect that Mary blamed him for Eliza's condition. He and Mary argued, and Bishop tried to reassure Mary that her sister's anxiety and confusion would pass with time. Mary did not like arguing with her brother-in-law, but she did not accept his logic either. "My spirits are harried with listening to pros and cons, and my head is so confused that I sometimes say no when I ought to say yes. My heart is almost broken with listening to B. while he reasons the case." She decided to take matters into her own hands. Fanny came to join her at the Bishop house, which made it easier for Mary to enact the desperate rescue mission she had appointed herself.

One morning in January, while Bishop was away, Mary, Eliza and Fanny boarded a coach and raced to London. Eliza was so nervous about her getaway that she bit her wedding band to pieces. In London, the women switched coaches and rode to Hackney, running an unpredictable path to throw off pursuit. They lodged in boarding houses under false names. Mary called herself Miss Johnson. She gave some thought to the baby they had left behind: "The poor brat! it had got a hold of my affections; some time or other I hope we shall get it," Mary said.

Meredith Bishop tried to plead his case through Ned. Ned was furious at his sisters but could offer Bishop no assistance. Mary, too, sought Ned's counsel, through Everina. Could Bishop legally force Eliza to come home? Ned raged at Mary, as did other family members. They all thought she had overstepped her bounds by whisking Eliza away from her husband and child. Mary stood up to them, but soon began to suffer stomach cramps and pains in her legs.

Meanwhile, the rain poured day and night. Cold winds raked the streets of Hackney. Each time someone called out in the streets below, Mary and her companions feared it was the authorities coming for Eliza.

The women and the Bloods struggled to come up with a more stable arrangement. Mr. Blood offered to take them in, but Mary knew the Blood house was too small. Mary's old friend Mrs. Clare suggested they might borrow money from Ned to set up a shop, but that was not likely because of Ned's anger at her. Mrs. Clare also said that she knew Mary had done the right thing, but that Eliza would eventually have to go back to Bishop.

As always, when Mary met with criticism, she became all the more determined to resist. She wrote Everina that she had not undertaken her current task lightly although she felt "some pain in acting with firmness, for I hold the marriage vow sacred."

But the cold weather and discomfort took their toll. As their money dwindled, Mary knew the three must find some work or they would be forced to return Eliza to her husband. In February of 1784, the Clares agreed to lend the three young women money to start a school. Starting her own school would give Mary her cherished independence. They found a suitable building in the village of Islington and bought books and supplies.

For several months, they struggled to attract pupils. Then a friend of Mary's, a widow named Mrs. Burgh, suggested they move the school to another village called Newington Green. Mary agreed, and Mrs. Burgh was able to use her influence to help them get an adequate supply of pupils.

Newington Green offered other advantages. It was a rustic village with gardens and wide fields. Mary continued to struggle financially, but found much to like about the pretty village scenery.

The move to Newington Green turned out to be a great piece of luck for Mary because she met some people who would be important to her future. The Dissenters were a group of intellectuals, writers and artists who often rebelled against conventional society. Like Mary, the Dissenters did not think tradition provided the answers for everything.

Chapter Three

". . . a world in ruins"

Through the window of her house Mary could see the chapel at the other end of Newington Green. Often, a short man in a proper wig, dressed neatly in black, left the chapel to make his rounds among the people. Eventually, she learned that this man was the former reverend of the Presbyterian Church. Dr. Richard Price was well respected in Newington Green, though his untraditional ideas had earned him some powerful enemies in England's political circles. Mary attended his church. He had retired several years before and preached only evening services.

Mary found Dr. Price to be a kind and tolerant man, who was open-minded toward new ideas. Children loved him. When he walked in the countryside, he stopped to flip overturned beetles right side up and to free trapped birds from nets. Dr. Price had a group of well-read friends and was always willing to introduce a new member to the group. Soon Mary was a regular member.

Price introduced Mary to people who were brilliant. A few were even famous. Price's circle included the scientist David Hume, philosopher Joseph Priestley, liberal theologian Andrew Kippis and the world famous American revolutionary, Benjamin Franklin. Mary made some exciting discoveries outside of Price's circle of intellectuals. Mrs. Burgh, the lady who had suggested that she move to Newington Green, gave Mary copies of her late husband's work. James Burgh had taught school in the village before his death. He had been inspired to write a spiritual treatise called *The Dignity of Human Nature*. Mary read the works of other Newington Green writers as well. Being around writers and intellectuals kindled the creative spark in Mary. She began to think of writing her own book. Perhaps she could express the ideas that made her view of the world different than that of other people.

The women of the group around Dr. Price were closer to Mary's ideal of a fair society than any she had ever met. They spoke and wrote as freely as men. Ann Jebb wrote articles on politics for the papers; Anna Barbould wrote poetry and essays on education. On the other hand, James Burgh did not support women's rights, and in fact wrote of the necessity of obedience to husbands. His opinions did not seem to have any effect on his widow's thinking. Mrs. Burgh did not write, but she did not hesitate to express her views on any subject, including politics.

Dr. Price was in his sixties when Mary first met him. While friendly, he still brooded over the death of his friend James Burgh. Mary had her own troubles. At first, she found herself unsuited for the task of teaching. Like her father, she tended to be impatient. Unlike John Edward though, she learned to be patient, at least with her students.

Mary faced many other trials in running her school at Newington Green. She struggled to attract enough pupils to

Dr. Richard Price introduced Mary to a circle of open-minded philosophers, politicians and writers.

support the school. On Mrs. Burgh's suggestion, she began to take in boarders. She did not fancy herself the keeper of a boardinghouse, though, and found the extra noise a distraction. Everina eventually came to join Mary, Fanny and Eliza, and to teach at the school. This sometimes created more problems; Everina had a short temper and sometimes took it out on the students.

Mary worked to keep her own emotions in check. Eliza was a lenient teacher who handed out sweets to students, while Everina was a teacher to be dreaded. Mary's style fell somewhere between the two. Teaching offered her a chance to put some of her theories in practice. She paid as much attention to the girls as the boys, and made both genders learn moral values. Mary did not hesitate to point out errors in pupils' work, and she sharply rebuked them for breaking rules of conduct. But she liked the trusting manner of children, the way they looked to her for guidance. The time for shaping minds was in the early years, she realized. Teaching was a great and noble responsibility. Mary developed strong ideas on the best way to teach.

Fanny's teaching was hampered by ill health. Mary could hear her friend coughing in her room. What would become of her dear friend? Fanny's suitor, Hugh Skeys, soon settled the question. In the winter of 1784, he sent word for Fanny to join him in Lisbon, Portugal. They would be married. Despite her illness, Fanny packed her bags and sailed to Lisbon in January. The climate in Lisbon was sunny and mild, but Mary worried about her friend anyway. She thought that Fanny's illness had progressed too far to be cured by a mild climate.

Fanny's letters from Lisbon were filled with witty observations and little jokes. Mary suspected that she was suffering, but Fanny seemed determined to look on the bright side. She jokingly described her new husband's affection. "I am sorry to add that he is too much inclined to pay attention to his wife than any other woman—but 'tis a fault a little time no doubt will cure," Fanny wrote.

The financial situation at Mary's boardinghouse and school was not so cheery. She lost one of her helpers. Then a boarder left. The situation fexasperated and depressed her. She wrote to Fanny's brother George Blood, who was in Ireland at the time. She complained that she was "plagued with bad servants added to the other cares that attend the management of a family . . . our affairs here do not wear the most smiling aspect."

George Blood himself arrived soon after and added to Mary's burdens. George was apprenticed to a lawyer in the hopes of learning enough to build his own practice. The lawyer, a Mr. Palmer, practiced near Newington Green. But, soon after taking George on as an apprentice, Palmer was arrested for forgery. George came to Mary's house for fear that he would be implicated. Mary had befriended George because he was her best friend's brother, but her feelings for him had blossomed into affection and loyalty. Soon after he came to her house, the bailiffs followed. Mary was prepared to defend her friend against the forgery charge, but the bailiffs told her they had come for a different reason. They suspected George was the father of a child of one of Palmer's servants. Mary refused to believe it.

"I suppose the child is Palmer's," she wrote, "or many fathers may dispute the honor." George left her house soon after. Mary wrote to him regularly. Her letters described a growing feeling of dread. "How my social comforts have dropped away," she wrote. "Fanny first and then you went over the hills and far away—I am resigned to my fate, but that gloomy kind of resignation that is akin to despair—my heart—my affection cannot fix here and without someone to live this world is a desert to me."

Mary continued to think that suffering had a purpose. She held strongly to her religious faith, though she questioned many of its traditions. The pain and depression she experienced were surely intended by God to strengthen her, to build her character through trial, as with Christ and the saints. She wrote George that she would "travel on the thorny path with the same Christian hopes that render my severe trials a cause of thankfulness—when I can think."

In September of 1785, word came from Lisbon that Fanny was pregnant—and that her tuberculosis had worsened. The letter also bore a request: could Mary come and stay with her until the child was born?

Mary was struggling to keep her school open. If she left, the parents would surely think twice about continuing to send their children there. Eliza and Everina had played little part in overseeing the school's operation, and could not be depended on to keep it running at such a rocky period. But Mary placed her duty to her old friend ahead of practical considerations. In November, she packed and boarded a ship to Lisbon.

Storms lashed the boat on its journey across the ocean and

through the Bay of Biscay. Mary wondered if her journey would end with her and the ship's other passengers at the bottom of the ocean. "The sea was so rough, and we had such hard gales of wind, the captain was afraid we would be dismasted," she wrote. "The water came in at the cabin windows, and the ship rolled about in such a manner, it was dangerous to stir. The women were seasick the whole time."

The journey lasted thirteen days. Mary arrived in Lisbon to find Fanny already in labor. The child was born underweight and frail. Shortly after the baby's birth, on November 29, 1785, Fanny died. After witnessing the death of her friend of so many years, Mary had little desire to stay in Lisbon. She soon boarded a ship for London.

It had been a depressing and helpless trip. And again on her journey back the ship sailed through violent storms. Mary thought the waves would capsize the ship before it arrived. Even in her fear, however, Mary maintained a strong moral vision. When the captain refused to allow the crew of a storm-crippled ship on board—he insisted there was not enough room—Mary astonished the sailors by promising to report the captain if he did not show them mercy. The captain relented and the thankful crew boarded.

After the ship sailed into London, Mary watched the dirty side of London roll past the window of her coach. She looked at the crowded, stinking streets, filled with sight after sight of harrowing poverty. How could her countrymen tolerate such misery and immorality? "She met some women drunk; and the manners of those who attacked the sailors made her shrink into herself and exclaim, are these my fellow-creatures!" Mary wrote of her experience in a later work of fiction.

Mary saw vulgarity, dirt and vice. This was the first time she had taken note of such misery. Forgetting her own grief at Fanny's death, she "mourned for a world in ruins."

The brutal injustices of the British class system, combined with the harrowing working conditions in the factories of the early years of the industrial revolution, created a depth of poverty and misery that angered Mary. There was a strong political element to her anger. Even after it lost the American colonies, wealth continued to pour into Britain from its vast colonies in the late eighteenth century. But most of the money went to about seventy noble families who held political power and flaunted their wealth extravagantly. Meanwhile, entire families labored from daybreak until long after dark in the workhouses. Some women never saw the sunlight except on Sundays. For single women, the financial struggle was even more difficult. With only a handful of ways to make a living, some desperate women turned to prostitution.

Mary found herself facing financial ruin when she returned to her school. Everina and Eliza had quarreled with one of the boarders, a Mrs. Disney, and the angered resident had stormed out without paying her rent. Her classes had dwindled. She no longer had the money to keep such a large house. She paid her debts until her funds dried up, turning down George Blood's suggestion that she flee to Ireland.

By spring of 1786, Mary closed her doors. She moved in with a Mrs. Blackburn, with only one servant, while Everina and

Eliza hoped to find work teaching or sitting with elderly women. Eliza left angry, convinced that Mary had never done enough to help her. Mary was never able to say anything to change Eliza's mind.

Amid all these bad tidings came one fortunate event. A friend of Mary's, the Reverend John Hewett, was convinced that she ought to write a book about the subjects she spoke so passionately about. He introduced her to publisher Joseph Johnson.

Johnson was the kindest of editors, a man who inspired his writers to use their skills in expressing their ideas. He often fed his struggling authors and was well known for the generous meals he laid out.

After meeting Johnson, Mary and some of the brightest people in England discussed and argued the issues of the times. Mary began speaking out about the ideas she had learned from teaching. She argued, for example, that girls should be educated in the same way as boys.

This was the idea Johnson urged her to put in her book. The chance to do just that sparked Mary's creative fire. She decided to title her book *Thoughts on the Education of Daughters* and dashed it off at a dead heat, writing as fast as she could push her pen. This was a habit that became one of her great strengths as a writer.

When it was completed, the book eloquently made the case for a number of ideas that do not seem radical today, but were shocking to tradition-minded people of the eighteenth century. Like boys, girls should learn logic, mathematics and independent thinking. Children should be guided by love and reason,

Mary wrote, not the fear of punishment. While most writers of her time tended to flowery sentences, Mary wrote in a terse, clear style. "It is only in the years of childhood that the happiness of a human being depends on others—and to embitter those years by needless restraints is cruel," she wrote.

Mary's years of teaching were not wasted. She had worked out her theories on her profession while still in the classroom. She would apply this moral vision in her future works.

Mary was excited and gratified about the publication of her first book. But it did little to help her support herself during the summer of 1786. It earned her only ten guineas. She was nearing desperation when the Reverend John Prior, another of her Newington Green friends, arranged a job for her with a wealthy family in Ireland, the Kingsboroughs. She left for Ireland in October.

Mary did not want to leave her life in Newington Green. She now wanted to spend all her time writing, not taking care of a wealthy family's children. She still longed for an independent life. When thinking of living as a governess for a wealthy family in a huge Irish mansion, she could see the walls of a prison in her mind's eye. At the end of the long journey to Ireland, her coach clattered to the entrance of the grand estate and the gates opened. She passed though "with the same kind of feeling as I should have if I was going to the Bastille."

Chapter Four

". . . her mind appeared more noble"

Mary climbed out of the carriage and walked onto the elegant grounds of the Kingsborough estate wearing a blue hat and a long greatcoat she had made herself. She was ushered inside, where she met the Lady Caroline Kingsborough's widowed stepmother, Mrs. Fitzgerald. Three of Mrs. Fitzgerald's daughters bustled past her as they rushed out the door on their way to market. She felt out of place in the mansion with its sprawling lawns.

She was introduced to the children who would become her responsibility. The Kingsborough girls lined up to meet her. The three eldest—Margaret, Caroline and Mary—were to be Mary's students. There was also little Jane and Louisa.

While the girls introduced themselves, Lord Robert Kingsborough walked into the room. He was a strong, handsome man, with a knack at making light-hearted small talk. But Mary felt he was sizing her up as much as meeting her. She studied him as well, and quickly decided that he was a shallow rake. "His countenance does not promise much more than good humor, and a little fun not refined," she wrote later.

Her first impression of Lady Caroline Kingsborough was even less positive. The lady of the house summoned Mary to an upstairs bedroom. Lady Caroline, Mary was told, was recovering from a sore throat. When she first entered, Mary could barely make out the woman beneath the satin sheets because she was surrounded by dogs. No one loved animals more than Mary did, but this display seemed absurd.

When she entered the room, the dogs raised a din with their barking, so that at first Mary could hardly hear her employer speak. But as Mary listened, she realized that the self-indulgent Lady Caroline was no fool. She was refined, well spoken, and well read. Mary discovered that her new employer had read more classic novels than Mary had. Still, Mary could not help but wonder: why did this woman, with so much time and wealth at her disposal, lavish so much attention on her dogs, yet hire strangers to care for her children?

Caroline Kingsborough was "shrewd, clever, a great talker ... a clever woman and a well-meaning one, but not of the order of being I could love," Mary wrote.

She was glad when the conference ended and the door closed on the yapping dogs in Lady Caroline's bedroom. Mary was shown to her own bedroom and found that the Kingsboroughs had provided her with beautiful, comfortable quarters. A fire crackled in the fireplace. Her windows opened on a spectacular view of Galties mountain range. Mount Galtymore, the largest, towered over the plain. Six lesser peaks—Temple Hill, Knockateriff, Lyracappaul, Carignabinnia, Slievecushnabinnia and Knocknanuss—clustered like a battalion around Galtymore. Clouds like crowns capped the hills.

Mary sat down and began writing letters to her sisters. Sounds from a room below broke her concentration. It was music! An Irish melody lilted up the stairs. To many people, and perhaps to Mary in different circumstances, the music might have brought comfort and cheer. But for reasons she could not quite understand, the violin music was the most melancholy sound on earth. It emphasized the fact that she was in a strange house in another country, with its own traditions and music and customs. Another point occurred to her as well. The musician was merely another servant, playing for the pleasure of his Lord. The class system of both Ireland and England stood here as firmly as the walls of the Kingsborough mansion.

Her duties commenced soon after sunrise the next morning. The children had planned to give her a harsh initiation. They mischievously decided they would try everything they could think of to annoy her. But Mary had learned to handle children. They found in her tenderness combined with a no-nonsense attitude. Later, the disarmed Kingsborough children confessed their intentions to rattle her as a new teacher. They swore they would make no more trouble. They were children after all. She had expected to be exasperated by this pampered brood. But they developed an affection for her that she returned. "The children cluster about me—one catches a kiss, another lisps my long name—while a sweet little boy who is conscious that he is favorite, calls himself my Tom," she wrote.

It did not take long for Mary to see why the children preferred her. Lady Caroline frequently shouted at them when they disturbed her, as she did at almost everyone who bothered her.

Mary had learned to control her temper, keeping it in check for her writing and for dinner debates with her friends at Newington Green. Lady Caroline never learned to make the compromises that were necessary for Mary to make in order to earn a living. The children began to see their governess as their protector. The eldest daughter, Margaret, formed a lifelong bond with Mary. Margaret also wrote of her loyalty to Mary years later. "Almost the only person with whom I had been intimate with in my early days was an enthusiastic female who was my governess from fourteen to fifteen years old, for whom I felt an unbounded admiration because her mind appeared more noble and her understanding more cultivated than any others I had known," Margaret wrote.

Lady Caroline initially reserved judgment on her new employee. She had been disappointed before. She soon realized, however, that this young woman had such a rapport with the Kingsborough children that it would be a shame to lose her. Lord and Lady Kingsborough began treating Mary more like a member of the family than as a servant. This was a departure from the household tradition. "The whole family make a point of paying me the greatest attention—and some part of it treat me with a degree of tenderness which I have seldom met from strangers," Mary wrote to George Blood.

Mary showed her appreciation for the good treatment by attempting to use her contacts at Newington Green to help Mrs. Fitzgerald's son. He was a wild-natured boy. The family feared great trouble if he did not change his ways. Mary wrote to her publisher Joseph Johnson, who was even then working to bring out her first book, *Thoughts on the Education of Daughters.* Could a clergyman be found to take in Mrs. Fitzgerald's boy, Mary asked. Unfortunately, Johnson was unable to help. But the gesture showed the respect Mary had come to feel for her wealthy employers.

But Mary could not refrain from passing judgment on the Kingsboroughs in her letters and journals. The vision of a world where women and men alike concerned themselves with important ideas remained an ideal from her days at Newington Green. The Kingsboroughs' lives could hardly have been farther from that ideal.

As the midwinter winds howled around the estate, Mary frequently found herself shut up all day with the women. As the men hunted or collected rents from tenants, the women prattled on endlessly about fashion and clothes. Mary sometimes thought she would go mad, as the Kingsborough ladies fretted for as long as five hours at a time about what to wear.

Mary continued to suffer from emotional turmoil. When Margaret fell sick, Mary was at her best, dutifully nursing her and giving out orders to those who helped. Mary was always most happy when she had a mission to perform. But when Margaret recovered, and the world of the Kingsboroughs settled into its familiar orbit around balls, boring topics of genteel conversation and social events, a deep depression fell over Mary. She wrote Joseph Johnson, describing a despair that seemed extreme even for the circumstances. "It is with pleasure I observe my declining health," she wrote, "and cherish the hope that I am hastening to the land where all these cares may be

forgotten." The premature deaths of her mother and her old
friend Fanny continued to weigh heavily on her mind.

Friction began to grow between Mary and Lady Caroline. A
young married man, a school headmaster named George Ogle,
began to visit. He and Mary were friends, having met on the boat
to Ireland. He enjoyed conversations with Mary. When he met
Lady Caroline, she insisted that Ogle flirted with her. Mary
suspected he had as well, but it mattered little to her. It was far
more important to the lady of the house, who did not like to see
any other woman upstage her.

To her credit, Lady Caroline frequently tried to build her
bridges with Mary. She took her to a two-day festival in Dublin
to hear the music of the famous composer, George Handel. She
even persuaded Mary to attend a masked ball. It was just the kind
of event Mary would have usually disdained, but she got into
the spirit of the affair, donning a black mask and playing the roll
of interpreter for another woman dressed as a native of a South
Seas island. And her employers allowed her time off from her
duties to travel and see her friends. The Kingsboroughs tried as
hard as they could to earn Mary's loyalty.

But the foundation of their arrangement stood on a premise
that Mary found fundamentally unbearable—that Mary was
their servant, although one of highest regard. Mary viewed
herself as an expert in the rearing of children, and bound only
by a contractual basis to her employers. She also began to realize
another truth about herself—that she was a writer.

Mary began to work on her first novel. It was called *Mary,
A Fiction*, and was to be closely based on her own life expe-

Lady Kingsborough lavished more attention on her dogs than she did on her children.

riences. It would also include characters based on the Kingsboroughs, including a very unflattering portrait of Lady Caroline. The Lady Caroline figure is a woman named Elizabeth, who likes her dogs better than her children and is jealous of her own daughters.

Mary hated interruptions when she was working. When the old Earl of Kingsborough arrived one day, the whole family and staff was expected to turn out to greet him. Mary refused—she was busy. Mrs. Fitzgerald and other members of the family went up to Mary's room and implored her to make an appearance. Did she not understand what a snub this would be considered? Mary did not care. She had her own affairs to attend to.

Mrs. Fitzgerald often buffered the disagreements between her daughter-in-law and Mary. When she had to take a short trip, Mary observed her employer with a heightened awareness of her own disdain. "You know, I never liked Lady K., but I find her still more haughty and disagreeable now that she is not under Mrs. Fitzgerald's eye," Mary wrote. "Indeed, she behaved so improperly to me once or twice, in the Drawing Room, I determined never to go into it again."

Lady Caroline tried some final measures to gain Mary's good graces. When Mary complained about the cost of buying clothes and hats, Caroline gave her one of her own poplin dresses. Mary refused the hand-me-down, although it was a fine garment. Lady Caroline exploded in anger at Mary. How dare she turn down such a beautiful present! The lady's outburst wore further on Mary's patience with her situation. Scolding her was no way to change Mary's mind.

The breaking point came in late winter of 1787. Lady Caroline planned to attend a ball wearing a splendid dress covered entirely in artificial flowers. The whole staff, including Mary, was expected to spend its days helping make wreaths of roses for the dress. The very idea incensed Mary. She wanted to finish her book, and here she was creating foolish finery for a rich woman instead. Lady Caroline did not know it at the time, but Mary would have her revenge through her writing. With every wreath she made, Mary pondered another decadent twist for the wicked and lazy character she was basing on Lady Caroline in the fiction she worked on every evening in her room.

While Lady Caroline did not know about the treatment she was receiving in Mary's fiction, she did not miss Mary's evident and growing contempt. She finally realized she would never make a reliable servant out of this independent-minded young woman, whose will matched her own. In August of 1787, the Kingsboroughs fired Mary.

Mary took the last of her wages and traveled to London. There she visited Joseph Johnson in his publishing company and home at 72 St. Paul's Churchyard. He invited her to stay. They talked into the night about what Mary could do next, how she would live and support herself. Mary was uncertain about her future, but a strange sense of excitement gripped her as well. Maybe she could actually make a living as a writer. At night she could hear the bells of the great cathedral, tolling the hours. Mary began to feel her own time had come, a time when she would be the master of her fate and no one's servant.

Chapter Five

". . . a most ingenious foreigner"

Mary learned a great deal about Joseph Johnson's world while sitting at his dinner table. There she met many people, mostly artists and writers, whose ideas were in conflict with the traditions of eighteenth century society. Johnson sought out such people, even as he kept the presses of his publishing house turning.

Mary discovered Johnson was a man of two sides. One night, Johnson might talk well past dark, firing her ambitions to write, even though few men in England took women writers seriously. Then the next afternoon Johnson would pay off one of his authors with little comment on his or her work, coldly holding back any hint of encouragement. Writers who worked for Johnson sometimes wondered what motivated the man. Was it a love of literature, or a desire to make money? Few earned enough to turn down the beef at his table, so the conversation was always stimulating as the hungry writers gathered to eat. After listening for months to the senseless prattle of her former employers, the Kingsboroughs, Mary relished the intriguing dinner discussions.

One of the young literary lights who sat near Mary at Johnson's table was a Scotsman named Thomas Christie. He had come to London in 1784, undetermined as to what to do with his life. A brilliant young man, Christie could have had a career in medicine or literature. He chose to write. At the time Mary met him, he was tall and so thin she wondered if he ate regularly. Christie's brilliant wit delighted Johnson, and convinced the publisher that Christie deserved a place in Johnson's court. Johnson set Christie up as the editor of *The Analytical Review*. The review also helped out Mary. Johnson agreed to pay her a small salary to serve as a contributing editor. This meant that she worked for the magazine when no project of her own took precedence.

Shortly after returning from Ireland, in the fall of 1787, Johnson presented Mary with a bold proposition. He would take her under his own roof until he could arrange to find a house for her. He would pay the rent. He fed Mary and let her sleep under his roof without a thought to what the neighbors might say about the situation. He also paid her the ultimate compliment of making her a part of his circle, the people he considered to be the brightest people in England. Later, he found her a house.

Mary moved into her new house at 49 George Street, near Johnson's own home. She wrote letters to her sisters Eliza and Everina that were charged with enthusiasm. Johnson's belief in her talents and character helped to hold off her bouts with depression during this period.

Johnson astonished Mary with yet another generous gesture. He provided her a servant! For the first time in her life, Mary could concentrate on her writing without worrying about routine household work. She soon was able to give Johnson the completed manuscript of *Mary, A Fiction,* the novel she had started while living in Ireland. She wrote Everina of her good fortune and her intentions, which included plans to write another book. "Before your vacation I shall finish another book for young people which I think has some merit," Mary wrote. "I live alone. I mean I have only a servant, a relation of Mr. Johnson's, sent to me out of the country. All this will appear to you like a dream."

Mary also wrote some lines in her letter to her sisters that could hardly have brought comfort to either of them. She wrote that while she remained devoted to them, they could expect to visit her "for a few months in the year." The invitation was a subtle hint that Mary would no longer consider herself the supporter and protector of her sisters. She had new goals of her own to pursue, and she expected them to make their own way.

Eliza took Mary's personal declaration of independence particularly hard. Mary, after all, had led Eliza to leave her own husband and family to strike out on her own. Mary saw things differently. She had helped Eliza make her own way in the world, as she herself planned to do. Mary failed to realize that her sisters lacked her talents, and could not as easily create as unorthodox a life as she had been able to do. Eliza's anger over what she considered to be Mary's abandonment of her lasted a lifetime.

In truth, Mary gave little thought to Eliza's predicament, or to anything else but her writing during the first months in her new house. Johnson published *Mary, A Fiction.* The book romanticized her life at the Kingsboroughs, and was peopled

Publisher Joseph Johnson provided Mary a place to live and gave her a job as an editor of *The Analytical Review.*

with slightly veiled real-life characters that portrayed her disgust at the pampered rich.

The heroine of the book is a young woman of high intelligence who is hampered by an inadequate upbringing. She feuds with her well-to-do parents. She marries, but finds herself unsatisfied with her marriage. She even faces trials in her relationship with her best friend, Ann, a character based on Fanny Blood. Mary Wollstonecraft named the heroine's mother Elizabeth, the same name as her own mother. But the Elizabeth in the book is clearly a caricature of Lady Caroline Kingsborough. Elizabeth ignores her children and lavishes attention on her dogs. She cares a great deal about what people think of her, but has lost the capacity to feel deeply about anything else.

Meanwhile, after her marriage, Mary finds she prefers the company of writers to her husband and develops a warm connection with an ugly, invalid violinist named Henry. She listens to him play beautiful songs on his violin. Their relationship takes a romantic turn, and the two share some passionate embraces. Infidelity was a shocking subject for the time. Mary tempered the shock by making Henry a dying man, hence less of a threat to her character's marriage. But the contrast between the romantic Mary, driven by her feelings, and Elizabeth, a slave to society's expectation, is the guiding theme of the book—and it is quite clear that the author's sympathy is with the character Mary. The book ends with Henry's death. Mary returns to her estates, and idealistically attempts to run it like a small society, breaking it into small farms so that the people dominated by her family can live with more independence.

Mary Wollstonecraft worked harder than she ever had before during the years of her association with Johnson. He had not published *Mary, A Fiction* before she had submitted her next work, *Original Stories from Real Life*.

Original Stories continues many of the themes she had dealt with in the novel *Mary, A Fiction*. The central character is Mrs. Mason, a teacher trusted with a class of neglected and spoiled children who know little about the suffering in the world. She takes them on visits to the worst sections of the city, so they can see the misery that poverty brings. At one point, she leads them along behind a man who takes them to his family's miserable living quarters. "A man with a sallow complexion and a long beard sat shivering over a few cinders in the bottom of a broken grate, and two more children sat on the ground, half naked, breathing the same noxious air," Mary wrote. "The gaiety natural to their age did not animate their eyes, half sunk in their sockets; and instead of smiles, premature wrinkles had found a place in their lengthened visages . . . they seemed to come into the world only to crawl half-formed—to suffer, and to die."

Mary lightened the gloomy sections of the book with descriptions of the class's field trips to the country, where they watch the crawling insects, the furred creatures of the woods, and are heartened by the songs of the birds. Mary preached her own deep Christian faith in *Original Stories*, but it was a faith unlike most Christian writers. God had not punished the poor wretches of the slums for their sins. Instead, mankind had sinned against the poor, with its greed and neglect.

Mary could not spend all her time locked away in her house

with her papers and quill pen. When she needed to get away, she would walk the short distance to Joseph Johnson's house, over Blackfriar's Bridge, through neighborhoods not much better than those she described in *Original Stories*. Before she reached the sanctuary of St. Paul's Church yard, she had to walk over a bridge littered with refuse and filth. She made her way through crowds of pickpockets, prostitutes, and beggars. People emptied slop pails from third story windows into pedestrian traffic. Mary literally had to watch and guard herself every step of the way.

Upon her arrival at her destination, life inside Johnson's house seemed like a different world than the harsh reality outside. His house was oddly constructed, with walls that did not quite meet at right angles. This caused the diners around his table to have to jostle one another for a position to be seen and heard. Mary was probably not too much bothered by the ritual, having spent her life maneuvering for the chance to be heard.

Many of Johnson's guests were egotistical, with very high opinions of their abilities. Sometimes this arrogance may have been deserved. Two great mathematicians, John Bonneycastle and George Anderson, joined the literary circle. Bonneycastle was a gaunt and gangly man, with a long face and teeth, and a laugh like the braying of a horse. But he was generous with his talents. He later helped Mary educate her brother James. Despite his upbringing in a small country village, he later became a professor at the Royal Military Academy.

George Anderson was an untrained genius. One day, as Bonneycastle was reading a mathematical journal, he read a letter from someone he had never heard of who had devised a set of solutions for an extremely difficult mathematical quiz the journal had published. Bonneycastle sought out the author of the letter. It turned out to be Anderson, who was a seventeen-year-old boy working in a barn with walls covered by geometrical diagrams. The barn wall had served young Anderson as his blackboard. Bonneycastle took Anderson under his wing and later introduced him to Johnson.

But no one dominated Johnson's circle or its conversations as did the Swiss painter Henry Fuseli. Born in 1741, Fuseli had once planned to become a clergyman. He was even ordained a minister. Yet he found the writings of the French Revolution to be more interesting and revealing than the Scriptures. This confused him and, much as Christie had, Fuseli took a while to make up his mind what he wanted to be.

Fuseli came to London in 1763, at a time when he was trying to decide between becoming a writer or a painter. He tried teaching for a while, but hated it. He made his living for many years as a translator.

Fuseli was a late bloomer in other ways. He married at the age of forty-seven, to a woman named Sophia Rawlins. A year later, his first great picture was hung at the Royal Academy. Called *The Nightmare,* it was a macabre painting of a demon crouching on a sleeping woman's chest. This work set the tone for most of his other paintings. Usually, they were portrayals of nightmare scenes that have kept their power to awe and shock viewers to the present day.

Mary soon learned that it was hard to get a word in edgewise when Fuseli visited Johnson's table, and it was nearly impossible to contradict him without arguing for the entire afternoon. Johnson warned Bonneycastle seconds before his and Mary's first meeting with Fuseli, when he heard the painter coming up his stairs. "I will now introduce you to a most ingenious foreigner," Johnson said, "but if you wish to enjoy his conversation, do not attempt to stop the torrent of his conversation by contradicting him."

Fuseli dearly loved holding forth on his opinions. He had a great knowledge of English literature, and Mary enjoyed hearing him talk. Much of what he said was mesmerizing, although she sometimes tired of having to keep her own opinions quiet in his presence. Fuseli's influence on her grew stronger as their friendship grew. Despite his faults, she began to feel a great affection for this man of ideas.

After finishing *Original Stories*, Mary put her own work aside for about three years. What was going on in her mind she kept to herself, but she clearly was stirring with the ideas she was hearing from her new friends. During this time, she devoted herself almost entirely to translating other writers' works and writing reviews for *The Analytical Review*. She earned some acclaim with her translation of the French financier and statesman Jacques Necker. This translation was a large task for a woman whose own knowledge of French was self-taught. Necker's ideas were often obscure. But her translation became known as the authoritative version in England. Meanwhile, readers began to snatch up copies of *Original Stories*, which proved far more popular than *Mary* had been. The book went

Mary soon realized it was difficult to express her opinions around the artist Henry Fuseli.

through three printings before the end of the century, a success for a book of its day.

Success proved the best medicine for some of the physical ailments that often plagued Mary. She suffered far less frequently from stomach pains, headaches, and depression when her work was going well.

By 1789, however, Mary had begun to grow dissatisfied with translations and reviews of other people's work. Her own standards for her work grew higher during her association with Johnson's circle. She privately considered much of what she reviewed for *The Analytical Review* to be rubbish.

Mary began to cast about for ideas for another work of her own. She knew she wanted most of all to advance her social ideas, but how? The answer to her creative quest would come in part from a source across the English Channel, where a French king's refusal to heed his people's pleas for help sparked a revolution that would provide her the inspiration for her next great work.

Chapter Six

"I cannot yet attain to Woman's dignity"

On July 14, 1789, mobs from the streets of Paris attacked and liberated the Bastille, France's most notorious prison. The Bastille held many prisoners that were enemies of King Louis XVI and was a hated symbol of the power of the kings and to some extent the Catholic Church. Although there had been movement toward the revolt for several months, this action ignited the political upheaval that has come to be called the French Revolution. The western world had entered a new era.

The uprising in France captured the imaginations of Mary and her radical friends. Most in Mary's circle of Dissenters considered the revolution an uprising of the underprivileged classes. They cheered the revolt as a long overdue refusal of the working people to be dictated to by the aristocracy. Other writers and thinkers saw it differently. They argued that merchants and businessmen, new classes of people not allowed to enjoy the same privileges as the aristocracy, were now insisting on a share of power in the government and society.

The French Revolution inspired strong passions. But the subject was dangerous. Some in the English aristocracy, who still held power in Great Britain, considered the revolution a serious threat to order in their country. But Mary's mentor Dr. Price did not worry about the danger when he enthusiastically embraced the revolution. On November 4, he delivered a sermon praising the French rebels. "I see the ardor for liberty catching and spreading," he said. The rule of kings would fall to the rule of law, Price continued, and the toppling of the French monarchs would ring in a new age of freedom everywhere. As for those who feared a similar outbreak of violence in England, Price offered them not a word of comfort. England's abuses of liberties might match France's if the current course continued.

"We are, at present, a great distance from it," Price said, referring to the possibility of revolution in his home country. "But it cannot be pretended that there are no advances towards it, or that there is no reason for apprehension and alarm."

Printing presses churned out copies of Price's fiery sermon and spread it throughout England and France. He had enumerated reasons for alarm that those opposed to the radicals took seriously. The strongest challenge to Price came from the Irish-born politician and orator Edmund Burke. Burke had defended the American Revolution, a courageous stance for a member of the British Parliament, but he found few of the virtues of the American cause in the French Revolution. He attacked Price's views in his work *Reflections on the Revolution in France*, as well as in *The Proceedings of Certain Societies in London Relative to that Event*. In these now famous works, he wrote of the excesses of the French mobs that he said were marking their path to liberty with a trail of blood. "In the groves of their academy, at the end of every vista, you see nothing but the

Politician Edmund Burke attacked Dr. Price's support of the French Revolution in his book *Reflections on the Revolution in France.*

gallows," Burke wrote. To keep liberty, one had to limit it, Burke argued. He urged the French to employ restraint in the search for a better society.

In truth, the French revolutionaries used the hangman's noose much less than a new killing machine called the guillotine. The device killed by beheading its victim with a weighted blade, and was invented as a more humane way to execute people than hanging. To Burke and many other English critics of the revolution, this atrocious device symbolized the bloodthirsty excesses of the French rebels.

Burke's fear of the mobs sounded like the voice of reason to many in Britain. Others disagreed with his views, and most of these people wrote letters to *The Analytical Review*, where Mary was able to read a large sampling of the radical opinion in England.

It became clear to Price and others that Burke's arguments needed to be rebuked in a book-length work. The question became who that writer would be. Publisher Joseph Johnson wanted it to be Mary.

Mary had mixed emotions about the project. She believed in the cause of the French people against the king and aristocracy. But she was not sure that she wanted to pour her energy into this book. Eventually though, Price talked her into taking up her pen against Burke.

Johnson's motives were partly motivated by profit. Whoever published the quickest reply to Burke's book would sell the most copies. He pushed Mary to quickly finish the task, hurrying pages into print as fast as she dashed them out.

Soon she was almost drained of energy. One night an exhausted Mary went to Johnson's office and told her publisher that perhaps she should not have taken the project. She was running out of steam. Even with the pages already in print, she said, he might do well to find another writer. To her surprise, Johnson put up no protest. He said he would gladly dispose of the printed pages and publish someone else, if that was what she wanted.

Mary pondered Johnson's unexpected answer as she trudged home. Johnson had been understanding, perhaps too understanding. Did he have someone else in mind for the work? Did he doubt her ability to give Burke the quality work that the radicals demanded? Johnson could be kind, but he could also manipulate his writers. Mary took his too-quick acceptance of her quitting the project as a challenge. When she arrived home, she took up her pen again. This time she attacked the work with a rekindled sense of purpose and, allowing for few distractions, wrote steadily until she finished the work.

The book, *A Vindication of the Rights of Man,* sold rapidly. The reviews were not all positive, however. Critics complained of her digressions from the stated subject, the revolution in France. Mary wrote as much—or more—about injustices she had observed as those that had sparked the French Revolution. *A Vindication of the Rights of Man* held forth on the general subject of political wrongs.

But when she attacked Burke for his defense of British institutions, Mary became more persuasive. Burke seemed to suggest that the French should seek a Utopia on which to order their new republic, and hinted that England was closer to such a place. But was England really such a place, she asked? After all, farmers went hungry for fear of breaking anti-poaching laws designed to protect nobles. Press gangs wandered the streets, forcing young men into the Royal Navy. The law protected those who inherited wealth far better than it did those who showed great talent. Protection of property, she charged, seemed more important to Burke than liberty.

"Security of property!" she wrote. "Behold, in a few words, the definition of English liberty . . . But softly—it is only the property of the rich that is secure; the man who lives by the sweat of his brow has no asylum from oppression; the strong man may enter; when was the castle of the poor sacred?"

Burke's defenders, and even some of those who opposed his ideas, thought Mary went too far in her attack. She even leveled some personal rebukes against Burke, who had kept the emphasis in his work on the ideas he put forth. But Burke had written his work to dispute Dr. Price's sermon, and Dr. Price was one of the first intellectuals who had believed in Mary. Part of the ferocity in her attack on Burke may have come from the respect Price had earned from her. She painted a vivid picture of Price from those days, when he had appeared a dignified and kindly man praying from his pulpit. "Is this the man you brand with so many opprobrious epithets? He whose private life will stand the test of strictest enquiry—away with such unmanly sarcasm and puerile conceits," she wrote.

Mary's book achieved just what Johnson wanted. She was the first to argue against Burke's ideas at length, and despite her work's flaws, it succeeded in arousing great passion in the reading public. The first printing came out anonymously, but the second carried her name as author. The world finally knew that it was an English woman who had charged so headlong into the hottest political controversy of the time. The second work countering Burke came from the pen of the famed revolutionary Thomas Paine, who had made his reputation writing pamphlets, such as *Common Sense*, during the American Revolution. Soon, Paine and Wollstonecraft's name became linked in the public mind.

Mary was suddenly well known among the intellectuals in England. She enjoyed the recognition and sense of achievement, but fame did not heal the ills of her personal life. Mary's celebrity actually heightened the envy her sisters Everina and Eliza felt for her. After all, Everina and Eliza, still employed as governesses, were doing the type of work that Mary had compared with being imprisoned in the Bastille.

Mary still sent all her brothers and sisters money, and helped to pay for her father's upkeep as well, although he still drank and gambled as hard as ever. Everina wrote that when she had last seen him, his beard was unkempt, his clothes ragged and his body had shrunk almost to a skeleton.

Mary's success weighed heavily in the mind of her new friend Henry Fuseli. Just as Mary reached the height of fame with *A Vindication of the Rights of Man*, Fuseli was gaining fame with his bizarre and often frightening paintings. Their works could not have been farther apart. Mary made her reputation through writings grounded in her reasoning ability and based on morality; Fuseli earned acclaim with art that tested the limits of morality.

The relationship between Mary and Fuseli had grown closer over the months. His marriage had little effect on his friendship with Mary. Mary considered his wife, Sophia, to be an intellectually inferior woman whom the painter had married for her physical beauty. If Mary's low opinion of Sophia or her close relationship with Fuseli bothered Sophia, she did not show it. Mary frequently called on the Fuselis, although she preferred to spend time with him alone. Mary did not think highly of marriage and thought that her relationship with Fuseli existed on a higher spiritual plane than the one he had with his wife.

Dr. Price died in April of 1791. The passing of the man she had so defended in her book did not lessen Mary's political passion. In fact, she was already beginning to ponder a work that would make an even greater assault on conventional wisdom.

In October 1791, Mary moved into a new home at Store Street in London. As she settled her household, she felt a new sense of energy. She wrote a painter friend that she was sitting for a portrait and contemplating a new work. Referring to the portrait she was sitting for she said: "I do not imagine that it will be a very striking likeness, but if you do not find me in it, I will send you a more faithful likeness—a book that I am writing in which *I* myself, for I cannot yet attain to Woman's dignity, shall certainly appear, hand and heart—but this between ourselves—pray respect a woman's secret!"

Chapter Seven

"It is time to effect a revolution in female manners"

Mary's new home on Store Street was in the heart of a thriving district of intellectuals. Because rents were cheap, most of her neighbors were artists, writers, and theater people. To the north lay country much like that in which she had been raised. Fields and farms stretched for miles.

Mary continued to work in her accustomed manner, fleshing out her ideas for her next work in journal entries and letters. She took inspiration from her dinners and discussions with friends, particularly publisher Joseph Johnson. The conversation around Johnson's table flowed as lively as ever, with some of the most important thinkers of the time thrashing out their work and philosophy right before her eyes. Mary Wollstonecraft was now one of the most sought after members of Johnson's group. She often joined Tom Paine to bask in the light of their shared fame over their writings on the French Revolution.

In early November of 1791 Mary had a chance meeting with a man who would later play a large role in her life. The philosopher William Godwin arrived at Johnson's door, hoping for the chance to hear Tom Paine speak. Godwin had achieved a small reputation for his writing, but his best work lay ahead of him. Mary and Godwin took little notice of one another at this meeting. Godwin even complained that Mary had talked so much he could hardly hear Paine.

Mary continued her friendship with Henry Fuseli and his wife, Sophia. The three attended parties together. At one masked ball, a Fuseli admirer came dressed as a devil and attached himself to the trio, perhaps thinking that his costume was in keeping with the painter's bizarre work. Fuseli laughed at the man, then told the devil to go to hell. The would-be devil grew petulant, complaining of his uncivil treatment. Fuseli withdrew as well, despising to hear other people's complaints.

Mary endured the presence of another devil. She had started work on her next book. This one was going to express her views on women's rights. She had easily persuaded Johnson on the merits of a book that would argue for an extension of the human rights that had motivated the French Revolution. She would argue that such rights should be extended to women as well. Johnson agreed to publish it but, as usual, imposed a tight deadline.

Mary opened her door almost daily to find Johnson's "printer's devil" waiting for the pages she had just finished. Sometimes it seemed that she was feeding a bottomless monster. But this was the book Mary had wanted to write all her life. It was no great challenge for her to pour the words out. Her pen had to hurry to follow her racing mind.

Like most of Mary's work, *A Vindication of the Rights of Woman* achieves its power over the reader less by its organi-

Mary was not impressed with the young William Godwin when she first met him in 1791.

zation than by the fury and energy of its attack on the injustices she perceived. Its main points are that men and women should have the same access to education and choices of profession, and that society should reward women for their minds instead of their looks.

A Vindication of the Rights of Woman drew on Mary's own experiences, and especially on the years she ran her school. While boys were taught trades and professions, girls learned how to please by dressing prettily and being trained to be subservient and to repress their opinions. But, she argued, the respect women supposedly earned by acting submissive was in reality only disguised contempt. Mary drew on other evils despised by London's liberals to make her point. Like slaves, she said, women were more like property than human beings. Marriage was not an equal institution, but one that gave men all authority over their wives.

What lessons did society teach girls, Mary asked. To be docile, polite, deferential, and most of all pretty. Girls learned to wear dainty and precious clothes to make themselves more attractive, and to cultivate nice manners in order not to offend men. "In fact, if we revert to history, we shall find that the women who have distinguished themselves have neither been the most beautiful nor the most gentle of their sex," she wrote.

And what could a contemporary woman expect in return for perfecting the lessons that men required of her gender? To become a domestic slave, at best and at worst, an object of desire for men. Such a woman was "the toy of man, his rattle, and it must jingle in his ears whenever, dismissing reason, he chooses to be amused." Such roles debased both men and women, she wrote, as slavery ruins the character of both master and slave.

The sins of people Mary had known in her life influenced the argument she made in *A Vindication of the Rights of Woman*. Her father set the example of a man who forsakes his wife and his duty to his children. Her brother Ned was the son taught to reason and provide for himself while his sisters were trained only to sew, cook, clean, and to be courted.

Mary also did not spare the "gentlewomen" of polite society. Mary named no one, but it was probably the lives of her former employers, Mrs. Dawson of Bath and Lady Kingsborough of Ireland, which prompted her stinging assaults on women who conformed to society's expectations. "I once knew a weak woman of fashion, who was more than commonly proud of her delicacy and sensibility," Mary wrote of Lady Kingsborough. "She thought a distinguishing taste and a puny appetite the height of all human perfection, and acted accordingly."

"I have seen this weak sophisticated being neglect all the duties of life, yet recline with self-complacency on a sofa, and boast of her want of appetite as a proof of delicacy that extended to, or perhaps arose from her exquisite sensibility . . ."

In Mary's estimation, such women had been reduced to the moral equivalent of lap dogs. She tied morality to her argument that women should learn to use their minds as well as men did. Mary was a strong Christian at the time she wrote *A Vindication of the Rights of Women*. One of her central arguments in the book is that reason is a gift from God, and that it is a terrible sin to allow only half the human race to exercise God's gift of reason.

She held to a chaste belief about sex, declaring it unacceptable even between man and wife unless for the purpose of conceiving children. At the same time, she flew in the face of traditional Christians with her attack on marriage. She was the first to use a phrase that would rouse the fury of clergymen and congregations. She called marriage "legal prostitution."

Mary insisted that to waste a woman's talents wasted a resource of society. Under the strictures of the 1790s, even an educated woman was a dependent being, unable to tend her financial affairs if her husband died, or even to choose a life outside of marriage. "How many women thus waste life away the prey of discontent, who might have practiced as physicians, regulated a farm, managed a shop, and stood erect, supported by their own industry, instead of hanging their heads surcharged with the dew of sensibility . . . How much more respectable is the woman who earns her own bread by fulfilling her duty than the most accomplished beauty!" Mary wrote.

Mary used her teaching experience to advance some remarkably farsighted views on education. She wrote of coeducational schools, where boys and girls would learn the same subjects. Education would be free. Rich and poor would dress alike. Children from five to nine would learn philosophy, natural science and astronomy, as well as the basic skills of reading and arithmetic. Such an ambitious course of study seemed outlandish to many critics.

Although she rejected marriage as an institution, Mary wrote about one unnamed married couple who lived relatively close to her ideal, probably drawn from the parents of her early friend,

Mary had little respect for the intellect of Henry Fuseli's beautiful wife Sophia, who posed for this drawing by her husband.

Jane Arden. If so, Jane's mother must have stood out among her peers in Mary's estimation. She even forgave the family their domesticity, for the wife's opinions counted equally with the husband. "I have seen her prepare herself and her children, with only the luxury of cleanliness, to receive her husband, who, returning weary home in the evening, found smiling babes and a clean hearth," she wrote. "I have thought that a couple of this description, equally necessary and independent of each other, because each fulfilled the respective duties of their station, possessed all that life could give."

Mary dared England's establishment in the most direct way, by calling for a "revolution" in a society that dreaded the word. "It is time to effect a revolution in female manners—time to restore to them their lost dignity—and make them, as part of the human species, labor by reforming themselves, to reform the world," she wrote.

"I throw down my gauntlet, and deny the existence of sexual virtues, not excepting modesty. For man and woman, truth, if I understand the meaning of the word, must be the same . . ." In casting down her "gauntlet," Mary referred to the old custom of throwing down one's glove as a challenge to duel or combat. And many political foes were quite ready to do battle with her over *A Vindication of the Rights of Woman.*

Writer Horace Walpole called her a "philosophizing serpent," just the type of writer to be encouraged by the Dissenters, and went even further in describing her as a "hyena in petticoats." Hannah Moore, another woman writer, dismissed the book even while expressing a determination not to read it.

Moore even defended the practice of keeping women dependent on men. "To be unstable and capricious, I really think, is but too characteristic of our sex: and there is, perhaps, no animal so much indebted to subordination for its good behavior as woman," she said. Her critics turned out parodies of Mary's work, such as one titled *A Vindication of the Rights of Brutes.*

Other readers, however, considered it a remarkable book, bolder in its demand for female equality than any other ever printed. Author William Roscoe handed out copies to ladies in Liverpool. Even some women who had previously lived in the manner Mary condemned changed their minds about their station in life after reading it. Lady Palmerston, a woman much like Lady Kingsborough, cautioned her husband that she expected to be treated as an equal. "I have been reading the Rights of Woman, so you must in future expect me to be very tenacious of my rights and privileges," she wrote. Poet Anna Seward called the *Vindication* "that wonderful book" and urged all her friends to read it. Even John Adams, a future president of the United States, carried a well-thumbed copy.

The controversy helped to keep the book in the public eye, much to the betterment of Mary's, and Johnson's, finances. Selling to friends and foes alike, the book became widely read throughout England, France and the United States.

Now Mary became one of the most widely known women in the world. The year 1792 marked the height of Mary's creative and persuasive powers. It was the year she had finally gained her ultimate success—the ability to live as an independent woman.

Chapter Eight

"I feel great pleasure in being a mother"

At the age of thirty-three, Mary had an audience that would read anything she wrote on any subject. Before, she had to write the books and articles Joseph Johnson thought he could sell. But with the acclaimed *A Vindication of the Rights of Woman*, Mary had created a following of her own.

Fame and notoriety caught Mary by surprise. Her family also had trouble adjusting to her rise to prominence. Mary complicated matters by seeming to forget that her sisters did not share her writing talents or the good fortune it brought. She wrote letters to them that must have stung, given that both still envied her. She wrote Everina of having turned down a marriage proposal from a man of great distinction. "Be it known to you that my book, etc., etc. has afforded me an opportunity of settling *very* advantageously in the matrimonial line with a new acquaintance: but *entre nous*—a handsome house and a proper man did not tempt me; yet I may well appear before you with a feather stuck in my cap."

The thought of Mary with yet another "feather" in her cap offered no thrill to Everina. She and Eliza grew gloomy in their jealousy and feelings of abandonment. They had always expected a great deal of support from their sister. Mary's fame irritated them. "I never think of our sister but in the light of one who has died," Eliza wrote Everina.

Mary herself felt more like a woman reborn. She was not only pleased with her success—she was buoyed by the release of more than three decades of repressed anger. She took a long-needed break from writing, breathing a sigh of relief at no longer having to confront Johnson's "printer's devil" squatting at her door. Johnson fretted about slowed productivity. He would have greatly liked to publish a sequel to *A Vindication of the Rights of Woman.*

Johnson was particularly dismayed, as were many of her friends, that Mary now seemed to be more interested in Henry Fuseli's works than her own. She became fascinated with his macabre paintings, an odd obsession for a woman who proclaimed strong religious beliefs. Fuseli's scenes conjured up images of the bizarre. He shocked audiences with weird interpretations of such Shakespeare plays as *Macbeth* and *King Lear*, then painted a horrifying vision from John Milton's epic poem, *Paradise Lost.*

"Our friend Fuseli is going on with more than the usual spirit, like Milton he seems quite at home in hell," Mary wrote a friend. She had fallen in love with Fuseli, as well as with his paintings. Then she ended any hope of their continued relationship by making a rather bizarre proposal to his wife, Sophia. One day in 1792, she called on the Fuseli house when Sophia was there alone. She calmly informed Fuseli's startled wife that she wished to move in with them. Mary would make no effort to intervene in their marriage and recognized Sophia's rights as Fuseli's wife, she said. But Mary insisted that she and Fuseli had a spiritual bond so strong that she could no longer live without "the satisfaction of seeing him and conversing with him daily."

Sophia refused to even discuss such an arrangement. She threw Mary out of the house. When he heard of her proposal, Fuseli made no attempt to side with Mary. She considered this to be betrayal. This incident ended his and Mary's relationship.

Now Mary's chronic depression replaced Johnson's "printer's devil" at her door. She seemed to suffer frustration in her efforts to find happiness with other people.

Mary decided in late 1792 to go to France. Perhaps seeing the French Revolution firsthand would rekindle her spirits and provide material for her next book.

During this time, Mary deepened her connection to two old friends, the American couple Ruth and Joel Barlow. Joel Barlow was a friendly, extroverted man who wrote occasionally. But his main occupation was that of a businessman. Mary disliked the fact that Joel made his living through commerce. She always considered making one's livelihood through ideas to be a higher calling. Yet the Barlows remained some of her closest friends. They traveled to Paris with her and would later come to her aid in the turmoil of revolutionary France.

Mary settled in Paris in the comfortable mansion of a French couple proud to invite a famed English writer into their home. But when Mary arrived in December, the couple was traveling. She found herself alone in the house at 22 Rue Meslay with only servants for company. The serving staff lived in quarters distant from her own, so she had no company at night. She found the solitude unnerving.

An eerie quiet had taken hold throughout Paris. The revolutionaries had captured King Louis XVI as he tried to flee the country. Now he and his family were imprisoned and awaited trial. Since the king's arrest, the turmoil had ceased. It was as though Parisians were holding their breaths, waiting to see what fate awaited their former monarch.

The day after Christmas 1792, Mary watched from her window as the king's carriage rolled past. Guardsmen surrounded his coach as it headed for the trial. Most observers, like Mary, watched quietly. Only the rattle of drum rolls broke the tense silence.

The scene burned itself into Mary's imagination. Watching the monarch ride past, maybe on his eventual way to an appointment with the guillotine, added to her disquiet. She wrote a letter to Johnson, cautioning him not to joke about the phantasms she imagined. "Nay, do not smile, but pity me; for once or twice, lifting my eyes from the paper, I have seen eyes glare through a glass door opposite my chair, and bloody hands shook at me," she wrote. Her visions read like predictions of the bloody terror that would soon begin in Paris. When she went to bed after writing the letter, she dared not blow out the candle.

Daylight brought brighter thoughts. Mary found comfort among her expatriate friends and French admirers. She began to take dinner at White's Hotel, the informal center for English intellectuals in Paris. The conversation about politics and writing pleased Mary. It was the same type of lively exchange of ideas she had enjoyed so much at Johnson's house. People listened with interest when she spoke. Already admired by French revolutionaries for *A Vindication of the Rights of Man, A Vindication of the Rights of Woman* had just been published in France. She felt great satisfaction that it was her writing and ideas, and not mere beauty, that turned heads at the dinner table.

It was at this time, when Mary was at the top of her intellectual powers and influence among European intellectuals, that she began an affair with an American businessman named Gilbert Imlay.

Joel Barlow probably introduced her to Imlay. He was the first to break the news of their fledgling affair, in a letter to Ruth, who had stayed in London. "Between you and me—you must not hint it to (Johnson) or to anyone else—I believe (Mary) has got a sweetheart, and that she will finish by going with him to (America) as a wife," Barlow wrote. "He is of Kentucky and a very sensible man."

Gilbert Imlay was a charming man who presented himself as a rugged frontiersman. He was thirty-nine, Mary thirty-four. Dark-haired, handsome and persuasive, Imlay had written two books—*Topography of the Western Territories* and a novel, *The Emigrants*. Imlay's writings contained some of the liberal opinions Mary so much admired.

At the time Mary met him, Imlay was a businessman—but the business he was about in 1793 was an act of treason for profit against the United States. He wanted to persuade the new French government to help create a war between America and Spain

by provoking the colonists in Spanish colonies of North America to revolt. He assured the Committee of Public Safety that a
sum of 750,000 pounds would be enough to ensure victory over
Spain. Many of the colonists in the lower states were descen-
dants of the French and, according to Imlay, were still loyal to
France. He was certain they would rise up in revolt if the
government in Paris encouraged them to do so. Imlay hoped to
profit off the war as a land speculator and as the middleman for
money used to arm the colonists.

Imlay could have been hanged in America for his plotting,
yet he told Mary that he wanted them to settle in his native
country. He charmed her with visions of what their life would
be like in the wilderness. He had affairs with women in the past,
he said, who had proven to be unfaithful. By the late summer
of 1793, they were lovers.

In the summer of 1793 the French Revolution entered a new
phase that is now referred to as the Reign of Terror. Because
the British government remained steadfastly opposed to the
revolution, it became dangerous to be English. Several of Mary
and Imlay's friends were imprisoned. She fled Paris to the
village of Neuilly, where she took refuge in a rented cottage.

The tensions between the French and British grew. Mary was
in serious danger of arrest when the French government ordered
the arrest of all British subjects living in France. Tom Paine went
to prison. English newspapers even printed that Mary had been
arrested.

Gilbert Imlay came to Mary's assistance. He registered her
at the American Embassy in Paris as his wife, which automat-

ically made her an American citizen. This action might have saved her life.

Mary became convinced that Imlay's devotion to her was as strong as hers was toward him. But he probably never meant to take her to America, or to marry her. Imlay had woven an identity in France that was almost entirely a lie. He was no frontiersman, as he claimed. He had been born not in Kentucky but in Monmouth County, New Jersey. He told people he had fought in the American Revolution, technically true, but his service had been brief. He rose to the rank of lieutenant, but called himself "Captain Imlay." If he did take Mary to America, they would have faced trials only slightly less than the perils in France. Imlay owed money because of land deals gone sour and faced criminal charges for trespass and for debts.

All Mary knew was that he was a gentleman during his infrequent visits to her in the Neuilly cottage. She wished that she could spend more time with him, but she believed him when he said that his business forced his long absences.

While Mary and Imlay pursued their love affair, the French Revolution entered a phase of violence. From June of 1793 to July of 1794 France's new rulers sent a steady parade of victims to the guillotine. One day Mary dared a visit to Paris. She crossed the Place de la Revolution where the executions took place. Standing under the platform of the guillotine, she stared at a puddle of blood staining the cobblestones. She began to speak out in indignation at the slaughter. Horrified bystanders begged her to be quiet—her protest could cost her life.

Despite the terror around her, Mary's life was blissful during

Dr. Guillotine's machine was considered to be a humane invention because it made executions easier and faster. It was used daily during the Reign of Terror.

these days of her first love for Imlay. From the cottage, she wrote to him about her happiness. "Cherish me with that dignified tenderness, which I have only found in you; and your own dear girl will try to keep under a quickness which has sometimes given you pain," she wrote. "But good night! God bless you. Sterne says that is equal to a kiss—yet I would rather give the kiss into the bargain . . ."

Imlay had to change his scheme to match the new political conditions in France. He set out with Joel Barlow and another merchant on a new plan. He and his partners would provide the French with badly needed products like grain and soap. He bought a house in the city of Le Havre, located on the English Channel. This became the new center of his business dealings. Mary moved to be with him. They lived as husband and wife for six months. It was a magical time for her.

Mary became pregnant with Imlay's child. On May 14, 1794, she bore a baby daughter she named Fanny, after her girlhood friend. She wrote Ruth Barlow about the joys of motherhood. "I feel great pleasure in being a mother," Mary wrote, "and the constant tenderness of my most affectionate companion makes me regard a fresh tie as a blessing. My little girl begins to suck so MANFULLY that her father reckons saucily on her writing the second part of the Rights of Woman."

But Imlay could not stay settled for long periods of time. He told Mary he had business in London. He promised to return for her and the baby. She should return to Paris. There had been a lull in the bloody terror. She should be safe there.

The waiting stretched on for months. At first, Imlay made

excuses for lingering in London. Mary's anger grew as she suspected he no longer loved her. In one letter she responded to his plea that his situation had changed and he would no longer be able to take her to America. "You find now that you did not know yourself, and that a certain situation in life is more necessary to you than you imagined—more necessary than an uncorrupted heart."

At last, she left France to meet Imlay in London. She hoped her presence would rekindle their romance. She discovered instead that he had taken another lover, a young actress.

Imlay did provide Mary with a home in London. He set her up in a furnished house at 26 Charlotte Street. He visited her there occasionally. Sometimes they both pretended that the bond between them still existed. But it was clear that he no longer had any deep feelings toward the mother of his child.

The breakup took its toll on Mary's emotional and physical health. She felt humiliated that all her friends knew of her affair. Perhaps this was the reason she took Imlay up on his offer to pay for her to take a trip to Scandinavia to settle some of his business affairs. She had little desire to make the social rounds in London while she was the subject of gossip.

The trip revived her spirits for a while. She arrived in Gothenburg, Sweden, in June and traveled through Denmark and Norway with her baby daughter. Away from Imlay and London, her mind cleared of its recent troubles, and she recorded scenes in her letters to Imlay. The wonderful clarity with which she described her travels showed that her writing had improved even as her personal life unraveled. But after the brief diversion was over, she faced the unavoidable reckoning. In September she returned to London and the weight of Imlay's rejection settled once again upon her. She fell into a state of gloom. All she wanted was an escape for her misery.

Chapter Nine

"Is this compatible with the passion of love?"

On a drizzly afternoon in October 1795, Mary wrote to Gilbert Imlay. She denounced his lack of conscience and wrote that she hoped her own death might help him develop one. She warned her former lover that she hoped her image would haunt him with guilt. "Should your sensibility ever awake, remorse will find its way to your heart; and, in the midst of business and sensual pleasure, I shall appear to you, the victim of your deviation from rectitude," she wrote.

Near dusk the drizzle turned to rain. The boatman ferrying passengers across the Thames River, downstream from Putney Bridge, must have been surprised at the arrival of a thoroughly drenched woman who asked to rent a boat in such weather.

Mary hired the boat to take her to Putney Bridge where she climbed out and walked up to the bridge gate. She paid the halfpenny toll and quickly hurried on. She wanted to get a good distance from anyone before she jumped. The bridge was equipped with bays so that foot travelers could stand clear of the coaches. Mary stepped into the bays and walked back and forth under downpour, deliberately drenching her skirts to add weight so they would hold her under the rushing waters. By the time she had finished, Mary must have looked almost like the ghostly apparition she wanted to be when Imlay next saw her.

Two thin rails separated walkers from the waters below. Mary gathered her wet, heavy clothes about her, climbed over the boards, and jumped.

The fall did not knock her out. Pockets of air billowed in her skirts, lifting her up enough for the briefest breaths before she sank again. She floated two hundred yards before a boatman saw her and rescued her. She was carried to The Duke's Head, a public house with a bad reputation. Eventually, friends were summoned to take her home.

When he heard of her suicide attempt, Imlay tried to make amends. He offered her money, which Mary considered an insult. He also implied that his new courtship was not a serious affair. It was only a passing fling and he had no strong attachment to the woman who now shared his house. Mary decided to make a last-ditch effort to win him back. She proposed that the three live together, much as she had suggested to Sophia Fuseli. Imlay had no objections and took Mary to inspect the house. But at the last minute he balked.

This final break again left Mary despondent. She did manage to salvage something of value from her affair with Imlay. She asked that he return her letters. As Mary pored over what she had written, she realized that the writing about her Scandinavian trip on Imlay's behalf could make a good travel book. She set to work on *Letters Written During a Short Residence in Sweden, Norway and Denmark.*

The book, published in 1796, marked a departure from Mary's

Despite her personal despair, Mary enjoyed a reputation as one of Europe's boldest and most orignial writers.

usual style. She left the letters in first person, although she had never written in that voice before. She allowed herself more freedom than in her previous works, using a simple and conversational style unlike the more ornate style popular during this era. She also demonstrated keen powers of observation that brought her trip vividly to life for the reader. "Gothenburg is a clean airy town, and having been built by the Dutch, has canals running through each street, and in some of them there are rows of trees that would render it very pleasant were it not for the pavement, which is intolerably bad," she wrote.

She carefully noted such details as Sweden's estimated population before painting this image of a seaside village. "The scattered huts that stand shivering on the naked rocks, braving the pitiless elements, are formed of logs of wood, rudely hewn; and so little pains are taken with the craggy foundation, that nothing like a pathway points out the door," she wrote.

For some time after her suicide attempt, she stayed with friends. She later settled at 16 Finsbury Place. Mary revived herself by working and walking, her lifelong favorite exercise. At times she lapsed into bitterness. Over time, these periods became shorter and less intense.

Mary rejoined publisher Johnson's dinner group and discovered that it had changed. The Barlows had left London, as had several of her other friends. Thomas Christie, former editor of *The Analytical Review,* had died. She did not feel as much at home among the new members of the group.

Mary Hays, a friend who loved meeting and entertaining literary celebrities, invited Mary to dinner to meet several prominent writers, including the philosopher William Godwin. Mary and Godwin had met years before at Johnson's house, but neither had been impressed. This time they paid more attention to each other and found considerably more common ground.

The two writers were both at turning points in their lives. At thirty-seven, Mary had suffered rejection and disappointment in her affairs with men. Forty years old, Godwin had spent most of his life writing and working out his political philosophy. He was inexperienced at relating to women.

While Mary was in France, Godwin finished the book he had been working on when they first met. *Enquiry Concerning the Principles of Political Justice, and Its Influence on General Virtue and Happiness* advanced several far-reaching ideas. In it, Godwin called for the overthrow of social rank based on wealth and for universal education. He also attacked the institution of marriage, as had Mary. He considered the arrangement a degrading relationship based on property. London's liberals enthusiastically embraced the work and pronounced Godwin the greatest philosopher of his age. Men of learning and young disciples began to seek him out at his home in Somers Town. Women wanted to know him as well, and he found their attentions flattering.

One day while out walking, Mary decided to pay Godwin a visit. She knocked on his door. It was a daring move for a woman of the time, but one quite in keeping with Mary's character. Godwin was smitten by the gesture.

At the time they met, Godwin was scholarly looking, with glasses, thinning hair and a huge nose. He was not handsome by most standards, but women often found him charming and attentive. Mary had regained her health and, although she had disdained mere beauty as a standard by which women were to be judged, men nonetheless considered her striking, with her brown hair and eyes, fair skin and pleasant voice.

The two had much in common intellectually. Both had built their reputations as political reformers. They centered their lives around writing, philosophy and intellectual discussion. And as they would come to find out, each was very sensitive to real or imagined slights.

Equality of the sexes was not one of the causes Godwin defended in *Political Justice*, but she quickly persuaded him that it was the right position to take. The two read each other's works aloud, and exchanged criticisms. They visited for tea and took long walks with little Fanny by their side. Mary convinced Godwin of the healthful benefits of walking. Before meeting her, he had walked only when he had an errand to perform.

Soon Godwin was infatuated with Mary. They carried on their courtship through the spring, and by late summer were lovers. But a fear of going through another experience like that she had suffered with Imlay made Mary doubt the possibility of romantic happiness. She sent her new lover a melancholy letter. "You talk of the roses which grow profusely in every path of life—I catch at them; but only encounter the thorns. Consider what has passed as a fever of your imagination; one of the slight mortal shakes to which you are liable—and I—will become again a Solitary Walker."

Godwin wrote back and begged Mary to not reject his love.

William Godwin as he appeared during the time of his and Mary's courtship.

"Do not cast me off," he wrote. "Do not become again a solitary walker. I will be your friend, the friend of your mind, the admirer of your excellencies."

Self-doubt and emotional fragility tortured Mary. One day Godwin's mail might bring an impassioned love letter, the next day there would be a bitter rebuke over some slight Mary perceived he had made toward her. Mary would write of her "tenderness of the heart" toward Godwin, refer to their bond as "sublime tranquillity." Then something would stir the old memory of rejection and she would turn on him. She once told him she wished she could undo all that had passed between them. He told her how stunned he was in a letter the next day. "You wished we had never met; you wished you could cancel out all that had passed between us," Godwin asked. "Is this—ask your own heart—Is this compatible with the passion of love?"

Godwin could be easily hurt, and Mary had a tendency to tease her friends. Godwin's mannerisms were easily mimicked and she could easily imitate him. But Godwin hated such teasing. They resolved one argument with an agreement—she would no longer mock him and he would not sulk.

In December 1796 Mary discovered she was pregnant with Godwin's child. This revived bad memories and fears. Would Godwin cast off the responsibility of fatherhood as Imlay had? But what if he did not? Could she build a permanent relationship with a man she had known only a matter of months? To make matters worse, both writers had condemned marriage. Mary and Godwin faced a philosophical dead end.

Mary was relieved when Godwin embraced the idea of

The marriage license of Mary Wollstonecraft (spinster) and William Godwin (bachelor).

becoming a father. They worked out a way around their opposition to marriage. They would forge a new kind of marital union—for the child's sake. While they would honor custom, each would continue to live independent lives.

Mary Wollstonecraft and William Godwin married at St. Pancras Church on March 19, 1797. Both proclaimed it a merely legal nicety, a compromise with a society they still wished to reform. Godwin signed the wedding certificate as "bachelor." Mary defiantly signed herself as "spinster," a derogatory term for unmarried women.

Both defended their philosophies, even as she moved to Somers Town with her new husband. They took great pains to explain to their friends that neither dictated the other's schedule or social engagements. Godwin vigorously tried to reconcile his former views with his new role as husband. He wrote their friend

Mary Hays to explain the predicament he and Mary had faced. "In short, we found that there was no other way so obvious for her to drop the name of Imlay, than to assume the name of Godwin," he wrote. "Mrs. Godwin (who the devil is that?) will be glad to see you at No. 29, Polygon, Somers Town, whenever you are inclined to favor her with a call."

Their defensive attitude toward the compromise that they made became a source of amusement to their friends. But after enduring a few whispers and jokes, the couple found that most of those who admired them for their talents and achievements continued to do so.

Chapter Ten

"A first rate woman"

Mary and Godwin began to enjoy the benefits of their marriage. Mary felt a new sense of contentment. She took part in the lively conversations at their teas and dinners. Writers, poets and painters listened intently to her opinions. The romantic poet Robert Southey, then only twenty-three years old, wrote of falling under her spell. She was "of all the literary characters, the one I most admire . . . a first-rate woman, sensible of her own worth, but without arrogance or affectation." Another romantic poet, Samuel Coleridge, praised her powers of conversation. The British essayist William Hazlitt noted with amusement that Mary was one of the few who dared challenge Godwin's cherished opinions.

The couple still argued occasionally, and each sometimes doubted the other's loyalty. In the summer of 1797, Godwin took a trip to the country with one of his young admirers. Mary stayed behind in London. Godwin took longer than expected on his journey and she became angry. Mary was also angered when he went to a stage show in which a woman wore a costume designed to simulate nudity. She later forgave him—he had been too late to see the offending show—but her feeling of security was very fragile.

A woman named Miss Pinkerton decided to test Godwin's commitment to marriage. She tried to maneuver Godwin into spending time with her alone, supposedly because she trusted only his opinions on literary matters. Mary found the intrusion quite annoying, even though she had made similar demands on married men in the past. She wrote Miss Pinkerton a note. While she would make no comments on her "strange behavior," she was no longer welcome in their home. She gave it to Godwin to read for approval. After perusing it, he made a single change, crossing out "strange behavior" and substituting "incomprehensible conduct." Miss Pinkerton troubled them no more.

Slowly, their trust grew. Godwin showed her a tenderness he had never bestowed on another. They took walks through the city and countryside, as he adopted her accustomed form of exercise. "I think it not right, mama, that you should walk alone in the middle of the day," he wrote. "Will you indulge me the pleasure of walking with me?" His endearment showed their affection. To the rest of England, they were daring and notorious radicals—to each other, they were "mama" and "poppa."

Mary began slow work on a sequel to *A Vindication of the Rights of Woman* in novel form. It was called *Maria, or the Wrongs of Woman*. Mary struggled harder with this work than any she had ever written. She was dissatisfied with every chapter she wrote. She rewrote chapters several times.

By late summer it was time for the new baby. Mary had written of the virtues of using midwives to help women in labor. In keeping with her views, she employed a Mrs. Blenkinsop to

The final portrait of Mary Wollstonecraft was made after her marriage to Godwin.

assist with the delivery. The call to the midwife went out early in the morning of Wednesday, August 30. Mary had assured Godwin of her faith that the birth would go smoothly. After all, Fanny had been born without complications. She told her husband not to come to her until she could present him with a newborn baby.

The delivery did not go smoothly. The labor continued until the early hours of the next morning when, finally, Mary gave birth to a healthy girl. Then, at about 2 a.m., a messenger arrived with bad news. The afterbirth—fetal membranes—had not come out as expected. The tissues were sticking to Mary's womb.

Godwin rushed to find a doctor and returned with Dr. Poignand, who worked at Westminster Hospital. He began the agonizing process of removing the membranes piece by piece. Mary bled profusely, and fainted several times. Godwin entered her room at 4 a.m. and found her barely alive.

Several doctors attended Mary over the next several days. She would seem to recover, then relapse. Godwin visited friends with medical experience, hoping someone would provide an answer for Mary's lingering weakness. On Sunday, the fifth day after her labor began, he returned to find Mary shivering from a chill. It was the first sign of infection.

The doctors prescribed remedies that did nothing to stop the progression of the infection. They had puppies brought to suck the milk from her breast. They advised Godwin to give her wine. Horrified at what seemed an assignment to trifle with her life, he nonetheless complied. "For me, totally ignorant of the nature

Mary Wollstonecraft was buried at the St. Pancras Church.

of diseases and of the human frame, thus to play with a life that now seemed all that was dear to me in the universe, was too dreadful a task," he later wrote. But he did as best he could, taking three hours to make her take the prescribed dose.

Mary talked with those who attended her, at times speaking calmly and clearly about her symptoms. Her coherence ebbed and flowed. By Friday of the next week, she suspected she was dying. Godwin also sensed that the end was near. Knowing he might have to raise two small children if she died, he sat by her bedside and tried to get a hint of how she would wish them raised. Mary, however, could no longer communicate.

Mary slipped back and forth between the states of wakefulness and sleep. On Saturday, she fell into a coma. Mary

Wollstonecraft died on a Sunday morning, September 10, 1797.

Five months after her marriage at St. Pancras Church, Mary's mourners laid her to rest in the cemetery. Godwin had a monument inscripted with a simple message: "Mary Wollstonecraft Godwin: Author of the Vindication of the Rights of Woman."

Mary's death came at the happiest time of her life. Godwin would never recover the happiness he had known with Mary Wollstonecraft. He married again, to a woman named Mary Jane Clairmont. The new wife's intellectual abilities did not match those of his first wife. Over the years, Godwin strained under the financial burden of raising a large family. He lapsed into a sad ruin of the fierce philosopher who had taken on the powerful in *Political Justice*. He constantly pressed his friends for loans. His fame gradually faded and he became the target of satire. He never wrote another book of the quality of *Political Justice*. By his death in 1836, he was remembered more for his personal failings than his literary successes.

The baby born that tragic summer of 1797 was also named Mary. As a teenager Mary Wollstonecraft Godwin, who idolized her mother's legacy, eloped with the married poet Percy Bysshe Shelley, one of the most famous writers in English history. Mary Shelley inherited her parents' literary gifts. At the age of nineteen, she wrote a novel about a monster called *Frankenstein*. Since its publication in 1818, the book has never gone out of print and has inspired countless movies and plays.

Fanny Imlay was not so fortunate. After her mother's death, young Fanny's personality faded from that of the bright, viva-

Mary's daughter, Mary Shelley, wrote the famous novel *Frankenstein*.

cious child to a melancholy, often depressed young woman. She always felt overshadowed by her younger sister, whom British literary society considered a likely genius from the time of her birth. How could she be otherwise with such brilliant parents? In October of 1816, Fanny committed suicide in a hotel room in Swansea.

During the years since Mary's death, her place in the history of women's rights has often been controversial. Her friend Mary Hays encountered a harsh reception when she attempted to carry on Mary Wollstonecraft's work. In 1798, Johnson published Hays book *An Appeal to the Men of Great Britain in Behalf of the Women*. This work encountered the same type of ridicule that was leveled at *A Vindication of the Rights of Woman*. Critics charged that she continued the Wollstonecraft habit of blaming institutions for all the sins of mankind. One critic even warned that Hays had damaged her chances of attracting a husband by writing such a book.

Mary's work was not always received positively, even by women who shared her ideals. But there can be no doubt her ideas were critical to the early years of the organized movement, such as the women's rights conventions of the 1850s and the American suffrage activists of the early twentieth century.

Mary Wollstonecraft's reputation rose prominently again during the recent era of feminism that began in the late 1960s. Almost all of Mary's work went out of print shortly after her death. But Mary's work was reprinted in the 1970s. Today, all her books are available, even the unfinished book she was working on at the time of her death.

Some of Mary Wollstonecraft's ideas remain controversial, while others have been adopted as society's standards. In an era when no woman was expected to speak her political views, she was one of the first to speak out against the unjust treatment of women in western society. This refusal to accept the inequalities of her era is the most remarkable characteristic of this courageous woman.

Timeline

1759: April 21: Mary Wollstonecraft born to Edward John and Elizabeth Dickson Wollstonecraft of London.

1763: Wollstonecrafts move to farm at Epping.

1765: Mary's grandfather Edward Wollstonecraft dies. Family moves to Barking at Essex.

1768: Wollstonecrafts move to Beverley, Yorkshire. Mary meets Jane Arden, who becomes her closest friend.

1774: Family moves to Hoxton in north London.

1775: Mary meets Fanny Blood, with whom she forms a very close friendship.

1776: Family moves to Laugharne, Wales.

1777: Family moves to Walworth, London

1778: Mary takes a position as a paid companion to Mrs. Dawson, in Bath, Windsor, Southampton.

1781: On news of her mother's serious illness, Mary moves back home to nurse her.

1782: April 19: Mary's mother Elizabeth Wollstonecraft dies. October 20: Mary's sister Eliza marries Meredith Bishop. Mary moves in with Blood family.

1783: August 10: Eliza gives birth to daughter, Elizabeth Mary Frances.

1784: Mary attends to Eliza, who suffers severe bouts of depression. Mary and Eliza run away and set up a school in Newington Green. Mary meets Richard Price, who introduces her to the group of writers and philosophers called Dissenters. Eliza's daughter dies.

1785: Fanny Blood marries Hugh Skeys in Portugal. Mary goes to Portugal to help her when her child is born. Fanny dies from consumption.

1786: Mary is forced to close the school at Newington Green. She writes her first book, *Thoughts on the Education of Daughters*, after meeting publisher Joseph Johnson. She travels to Ireland to work as governess to Lord and Lady Kingsborough at Mitchelstown, County Cork.

1787: Mary accompanies Kingsboroughs to Bristol, where she is dismissed. She moves back to London, where Johnson encourages her to write.

1788: *Mary, a Fiction* and *Original Stories* are published. Johnson and Thomas Christie found *The Analytical Review*, for which Mary writes reviews.

1789: July 14: Fall of Bastille begins French Revolution. In November, Price delivers sermon praising revolution.

1790: Edmund Burke attacks Price's views in *Reflections on the Revolution in France*. Mary writes spirited answer to Burke in *A Vindication of the Rights of Man*.

1792: Publication of *A Vindication of the Rights of Woman*. Mary travels to France.

1793: King Louis XVI of France is executed. Mary meets American Gilbert Imlay, with whom she falls in love. The French revolutionaries begin a reign of terror in June. Mary becomes pregnant, and is registered as Imlay's wife at the American Embassy. William Godwin writes *Political Justice*.

1794: May 14: Mary gives birth to daughter, Fanny Imlay. In April, Mary moves back to London. In June, she goes to Scandinavia on business for Imlay, a journey which gives her material for *Letters Written During a Short Residence in Sweden, Norway, and Denmark*. She attempts to commit suicide in October by jumping off Putney Bridge into Thames.

1796: Mary meets Imlay for last time in March. She begins a relationship with Godwin in July.

1797: Mary learns in February that she is again pregnant. In March, Mary marries Godwin in St Pancras church. August 30: Mary gives birth to second daughter, Mary Wollstonecraft Godwin. September 10: Mary Wollstonecraft dies from illnesses related to childbirth.

Major Works

Thoughts on the Education of Daughters (1786)
Mary, a Fiction (1788)
Original Stories from Real Life (1788)
A Vindication of the Rights of Man (1791)
A Vindication of the Rights of Woman (1792)
*Letters Written During a Short Residence in Sweden,
Norway and Denmark* (1796)
The Wrongs of Woman, or Maria (1798)

Bibliography

Jean Detre, *A Most Extraordinary Pair: Mary Wollstonecraft and William Godwin* (Doubleday & Company, Inc., Garden City, New York, 1975)

Eleanor Flexnor, *Mary Wollstonecraft* (Coward, McGann & Geogheghan, Inc., New York, 1972)

William Godwin, edited with preface, introduction and bibliographical note by W. Clark Durant, *Memoirs of Mary Wollstoncecraft* (London and New York, 1927)

Emily Sunstein, *A Different Face: The Life of Mary Wollstonecraft* (Harper & Row, New York, Evanston, San Francisco, London, 1975)

Claire Tomalin, *The Life and Death of Mary Wollstonecraft*, (Harcourt Brace Jovanovich, New York and London, 1974)

Mary Wollstonecraft, *The Works of Mary Wollstonecraft*, Volumes 1-7 (New York University Press, Washington Square, New York, 1989)

Sources

Chapter One
"I must have first place or none"

14 "I once thought myself worthy of your friendship" Eleanor Flexner, *Mary Wollstonecraft*, Coward, McCann & Geoghegan, Inc., New York, 1972, 24.

14 "I am a little singular in my thought of love" ibid.

15 "...a young woman of slender and elegant form" William Godwin, edited by Ralph M. Wordle, *Memoirs of Mary Wollstonecraft*, London and New York, 1927, 18.

15 "... a friend, whom I love better than all the world beside" Flexner, 26.

Chapter Two
"Pain and disappointment have constantly attended me"

19 "...whether in or out of the Season" Flexner, 32.

19 "All the damsels set their caps" Emily Sunstein, *A Different Face: The Life of Mary Wollstonecraft*, Harper & Row, New York, Evanston, San Francisco, London, 1975, 66.

20 "Pain and disappointment have constantly attended me" Flexner, 35.

20 "The happiness of my family" Flexner, 36.

21 "A little patience" Flexner, 37.

22 "She has not had a violent fit of frenzy" Sunstein, 81.

22 "My spirits are harried with listening to pros and cons" Sunstein, 83.

23 "The poor brat!" Claire Tomalin, *The Life and Death of Mary Wollstonecraft*, Harcourt Brace Jovanovich, New York and London, 1974, 26.

24 "...some pain in acting with firmness" Tomalin, 27.

60 "Is this the man" Wollstonecraft, *A Vindication of the Rights of Men* from *Works, Vol. 5*, 19.

62 "I do not imagine" Flexner, 147.

Chapter Seven
"How much more respectable is the woman who earns her own bread"

66 "In fact, if we revert to history" Wollstonecraft, *A Vindication of the Rights of Woman* from *Works, Vol. 5*, 98.

66 "the toy of man, his rattle" *A Vindication of the Rights of Woman*, 102.

67 "I once knew a weak woman" *A Vindication fo the Rights of Woman*, 112.

68 "How many women thus waste" *A Vindication of the Rights of Woman*, 219.

70 "I have seen her prepare herself" *A Vindication of the Rights of Woman*, 213.

70 "I throw down my gauntlet" *A Vindication of the Rights of Woman*, 120.

71 "To be unstable and capricious" Flexner, 165.

71 "I have been reading" Tomalin, 110.

Chapter Eight
"I feel great pleasure in being a mother"

72 "Be it known to you" Flexner, 169.

73 "I never think of our sister" Flexner, 168.

73 "Our friend Fuseli" Flexner, 173.

75 "Nay, do not smile" Sunstein, 230.

76 "Between you and me" Flexner, 181.

80 "Cherish me with that dignified tenderness" Sunstein, 244.

80 "I feel great pleasure" Sunstein, 257.

81 "You find now" Flexner, 199.

Chapter Nine
"Is this compatiable with the passion of love?"

83 "Should your sensibility" Sunstein, 291.

86 "Gothenburg is a clean, airy town" Wollstonecraft, *Letters Written During a Short Residence in Sweden, Norway and Denmark*, edited and introduction by Carol H. Poston (University of Nebraska Press, Lincoln & London, 1976), 19.

86 "The scattered huts" *Letters*, 25.

88 "You talk of the roses" Jean Detre, *A Most Extraordinary Pair: Mary Wollstonecraft and William Godwin* (Doubleday & Company, Inc., Garden City, New York, 1975), 39.

90 "Do not cast me off" Detre, 40.

90 "You wished we had never met" Detre, 182.

92 "In short, we found that there was no other way" Tomalin, 214.

Chapter Ten
"A first rate woman"

94 "I think it not right" Detre, 299.

96 "For me, totally ignorant" Flexner, 252.

Index
